She's So Funny

Angie —
Get Better
Soon.
We love you.

mom,
Anthony &
Debbie

Other books edited by Judy Brown

Joke Soup

Joke Stew

The Funny Pages

Jokes to Go

She's So Funny

1,768 of the Best Jokes
from Women Comedians

Edited by
JUDY BROWN

**Andrews McMeel
Publishing**

Kansas City

04 05 06 07 08 EDB 10 9 8 7 6 5 4 3 2 1

ISBN: 0-7407-4166-7

Library of Congress Control Number: 2003067450

judybrowni@usa.net

ATTENTION SCHOOLS AND BUSINESSES

Andrews McMeel books are available at quantity discounts with bulk purchase for educational, business, or sales promotional use. For information, please write to: Special Sales Department, Andrews McMeel Publishing, 4520 Main Street, Kansas City, Missouri 64111.

Acknowledgments

First and foremost, I'd like to thank a half century of female comedians who had the ovaries to stand up, speak their minds, and make us laugh.

I couldn't have compiled this book without the discerning wit of two assistants: Andi Rhoads and Jeanie Dietz, who are two crackerjack comedy writers in their own right. My editor, Jean Lucas, gets snaps for supporting this project from the first (and for agreeing to toss the first cover designed for the book—don't ask). Comedy Central and HBO also get a nod for giving funny women airtime (even if both seem to give a disproportionate amount to the funny guys). *Gracias* to the Improv in Hollywood and the other comedy clubs who give funny gals stage time (even if they sometimes seem to . . . oh, you get my drift). *Mucho gracias* to my female standup comedy students for keeping me in fresh laughter and for continuing the tradition of women's satire.

Introduction

Women want men, careers, money, children, friends, luxury, comfort, independence, freedom, respect, love, and three-dollar pantyhose that won't run.

—PHYLLIS DILLER

I'm just a person trapped inside a woman's body.

—ELAYNE BOOSLER

Although this comedy collection includes many of the best jokes from female comedians of the last fifty years, never fear—you'll find the laughs as tasty and fresh-baked as today's loaf from your bread machine.

A half century ago, American standup went through a merry metamorphosis from the old-fashioned story joke to controversial and conversational comedy. Lenny Bruce most famously joked about real issues in sex and race, and Bill Cosby was among the first black comedians to make a mainstream (read: white) audience laugh without having to demean himself.

And then a thirty-seven-year-old mother of five named Phyllis Diller stood up and made the daily concerns of women fodder for cathartic laughter: "Housework can't kill you, but why take a chance?"

Diller's records went gold and paved the way for a black female comedian to produce two dozen best-selling albums. The grandmotherly Moms Mabley, who refused to act her age, said, "There ain't nothing an old man can do but bring me a message from a young one."

The '60s also proved golden for funny girls like Totie Fields who said, "Happiness is finding a book that's three weeks overdue, and you're not." The redoubtable Joan Rivers dealt with the sexual revolution: "There's a double standard, even today. A man can sleep around and sleep around, and nobody asks any questions. A woman, you make nineteen or twenty mistakes, right away you're a tramp."

In the '70s, Elayne Boosler was one of many new female comedians who refused to succumb to self-deprecating jokes. "There's no leeway for a woman's looks," she said. "You never see a man walking down the street with a woman who has a little potbelly and a bald spot."

Elayne was the first female comic to film her own '80s cable special. She sold it to Showtime, and it became a ratings bonanza, effectively opening up TV to funny women such as Roseanne Barr. Roseanne's housewife jokes had a feminist, blue-collar bent, and her eponymous show helped refashion the sitcom with lines such as, "Husbands think we should know where everything is, like the uterus is a tracking device. He asks me, 'Roseanne, do we have any Chee-tos left?' Like he can't go over to that sofa cushion and lift it himself."

The '90s and the turn of the new century saw the arrival of alternative-attitude girls like Janeane Garofalo, who said, "I guess I just prefer to see the dark side of things. The glass is always half empty. And cracked. And I just cut my lip on it. And chipped a tooth." The coming-out party of Ellen DeGeneres on network TV made history. "I was raised around hetero-sexuals. That's where us gay people come from: you heterosexuals." Wanda Sykes was all over the dial, cracking wise on everything from marriage to sports and politics: "The president has done pretty much everything I expected him to do. The economy is in the toilet, we're at war, and everything is on fire." Margaret Cho made her own explicit movies that tackled, and then tickled, sex and racism. "I was walking down the street and this man actually calls me a chink! I was so mad: Chinks are Chinese; I'm Korean—I'm a gook. If you're going to be a racist, at least get the terminology correct. Okay, Bubba?"

All of these ladies make me look forward to what funny females will stand up and say for the *next* fifty years.

a, b, c

Abortion

I say to this dude with a "Stop Abortion" picket sign, "I have the answer to abortion: Shoot your dick. Take that tired piece of meat down to the ASPCA and let 'em put it to sleep."

—WHOOPI GOLDBERG

I'm getting an abortion. I don't need one, but I feel that as an American I should exercise that right before it gets taken away.

—BETSY SALKIND

My grandmother used to say that she was pro-choice because she was pro-women. I think it was because she just couldn't see another generation borrowing money from her.

—LAURA KIGHTLINGER

Addiction

I went on a hardcore drinking and smoking binge. It lasted right about nine months. And then, as soon as I was born, I was like, "Whew! Do not go in *there*."

—TIG

It's not my fault I have an addictive personality, because pregnant women in the 1950s didn't realize the stuff they did had any effect on the babies who were inside them. So my mother drank and smoked and carried on like every other pregnant Texas woman did. Mom told me I cried every day at five o'clock in the afternoon for six weeks after I was born. Well hello, Mother: It was the cocktail hour and I wanted my martini and cigarettes. I'd been getting them for nine months straight and all of a sudden I'm cut off from alcohol and nicotine. No wonder I cried, "Hey, where's the bar? And what's with that *Rock-a-Bye Baby* crap? I like Frank Sinatra!"

—SALLY JACKSON

I'm addicted to chocolate. I snort cocoa.

—MARILYN

Adoption

I became a mom six months ago. I adopted a highway. I'm trying to teach it to pick up after itself.

—NANCY JO PERDUE

I adopted a baby. I wanted a highway, but it was a lot of red tape.

—MARGARET SMITH

Advertising

A lot of people are concerned about truth in advertising, and I have to agree. Have you seen the paper towel commercial where the little boy tries to pour himself a drink, makes a huge mess, and the mom just smiles and cleans it up with one magical swipe? I don't know about the rest of you, but my mom had a different reaction. Obviously, we were buying the wrong paper towels.

—LORI GIARNELLA

I can't watch those Sally Struthers commercials where you can adopt a kid for sixty cents a day, because I feel so guilty. I have the money, but I know I wouldn't write the little fellow. Maybe if he had a cell phone, I'd call him.

–KATHLEEN MADIGAN

Aging

As I get older I realize it is the small things that make us happy. But I don't know if that's wisdom from age or the constant barrage of life's disappointments that make you set the bar really low.

—LAURA HAYDEN

I'm at an age where I should get in shape, but it's probably not going to happen. Quite frankly, I'm so lazy I'd drive to my bathroom if I could.

—MICHELE BALAN

Sex in your twenties, "Yes, yes, yes—again." Sex in your thirties: "Ow, my hip."

—CAROLINE RHEA

I'm getting older and I'm thinking about having my eggs frozen. Well, just the egg whites. I'm trying to cut back on my cholesterol.

—BRENDA PONTIFF

I'm at the "ma'am" stage of life. But you shouldn't be called "ma'am" until you've had that first mammogram.

—MARGARET SMITH

My sister Kathryn has some crazy ideas about getting older. After forty years as a brunette, when her hair turned white she decided that she'd become an albino. Yeah, Sis, and your wrinkles mean you're a shar-pei.

—DARYL HOGUE

I'm getting older so I've started to smile more because I want the crow's-feet to go up.

—SIMONE ALEXANDER

They say that you learn something new every day. But I'm at the age where I unlearn something new every day.

—JANICE HEISS

I used to be able to wave "bye-bye" and that was it. Now my upper arm will keep waving good-bye for an hour after I've lost interest.

—MEG MALY

You know you're getting old when you're more attractive hanging upside down.

—CATHY LADMAN

Making love used to make my toes curl; now it just gives me foot cramps.

—KATHIE DICE

Do you ever wonder if you really have arthritis, or is someone somewhere just having fun with a voodoo doll that happens to look like you?

—ROXANE LARIMORE

I'm now old enough to personally identify every object in antique stores.

—ANITA MILNER

I don't know how you feel about old age, but in my case I didn't even see it coming. It hit me from the rear.

—PHYLLIS DILLER

Terrible things happen when you age. I got a lymphoma on my shoulder. My shoulder. As if the fat formed a gang, went on a tour of my body, got to my ass, and said, "There's no room here," and then decided to hang out on my shoulder like a fat guardian angel to make sure I eat more fries, chips, and ice cream.

—MIMI GONZALEZ

There are all these magazine articles pushing the joys of senior sex. Oh sure, especially for my mother. "Can you try not to move much? I have vertigo and tend to get dizzy very easily. And we should leave some water by the bed because my medication makes me dehydrated. Can my aide stay in the room in case I need to get up during the act?"

—JUDY GOLD

The older you get, the higher you wear your underwear. Like rings on a tree. Eighty, ninety years old, your breasts are inside them. When you die, they just pull them up over your head.

—MARGARET SMITH

Alone

Remember, we're all in this alone.

—LILY TOMLIN

The other night I was home by myself and all the lights went out. I absolutely freaked out. I thought, "There's a guy in the basement, he flipped a switch, and he's coming up to kill me." Then I looked out the window and saw the lights in the whole neighborhood were out. I was relieved because I thought, "Maybe he'll start at the end of the block."

—PAULA POUNDSTONE

I like to live alone; you never have to clean up. I find things in the refrigerator, I figure out what they used to be.

—ELAYNE BOOSLER

Ambition

I used to be driven, but I pulled over.

—HEIDI JOYCE

Anal Retentive

I'm anal retentive. Oh, yeah, like none of you are. You're the anal-retentive one in the relationship if you sound like this when you're just standing around the apartment: "Does that go there? Is that just going to pick itself up? Weren't these alphabetized when I left this morning?"

—SUZANNE WESTENHOEFER

Ancestors

Ever since the caveman days, men have been the hunters while women have been the hinters. The first word spoken was by a woman; it was "Ahem." And about ten thousand years later, the man said, "What?"

—DEBBIE KASPER

I never understand people who brag about how long their family has been in the United States. "My family came over on the Mayflower." "Really? My family came over on Mileage Plus."

—SIMONE ALEXANDER

I'm descended from a very long line my mother once foolishly listened to.

—PHYLLIS DILLER

Anesthetics

Can you imagine what a nightmare it must have been before they invented painkillers? What did they do, have a guy bite a bullet? They could have done better than that. Bring in a big-breasted woman. That would distract any man. Stick a knife through their arm, they see those big breasts, they don't feel a thing.

—JOY BEHAR

Animals

If only someone would do for cows what Bambi did for deer. Cows have been in films, but they haven't starred. I'm still willing to eat a species that is only a supporting player.

—PAULA POUNDSTONE

I love animals, especially with gravy.

—CYNDI STILES

I read that when rabbits are having sex, the male rabbit screams, rolls over on his side, and faints. That's reassuring. Because now when I'm driving my car and see a rabbit on the side of the road, I know he's not dead, he just had a date.

—CATHY LADMAN

Anniversaries

My husband and I celebrated our thirty-eighth wedding anniversary. You know what I finally realized? If I had killed the man the first time I thought about it, I'd have been out of jail by now.

—ANITA MILNER

It's really hard with lesbian relationships to know when your anniversary date is. Is it your first date? The first time you go to bed together? Is it the day you move in? Lucky for my girlfriend and me, all those things happened at the same time.

—LYNDA MONTGOMERY

Answering Machines

My mother is really annoying. I just called and the message on her answering machine is two hours long and like the first draft of an autobiography, "You have reached 555-4748. I live at 310 Gibson Boulevard. On Tuesday from 8 to 11:30 I go to bingo at the synagogue. The money is in the top drawer of the dresser. The keys are in the ..." Ma, shut up!

—JUDY GOLD

I bought my father an answering machine. He still hasn't figured out how to leave an outgoing message. You call my father's house . . . ring, ring, ring, click, "Goddamn it, Mary, how in the hell do you use this stupid piece of shit? Come over here and look and see if you can help me with the . . . beep!"

—ROSIE O'DONNELL

Neither of my parents understands how an answering machine works. When my mother leaves me a message she's actually trapped inside the machine. It is just like a desperate cry. "Carol? Carol? Carol? Are you there? Carol? I'm in the machine." And my father's even worse. He leaves me these messages, "Uh, tell her that her father called."

—CAROLINE RHEA

An answering machine is like the stupidest gift to give your parents. No one ever calls them except for their kids. My mother put the appropriate message on the machine: "Look, we're not here right now. If you'd like to leave a message, leave one. If you don't want to leave one, don't. We're not going to be making decisions for you anymore. So make up your own goddamn mind. Thank you."

—JUDY GOLD

The technological advance I wish I could get is an addition for my answering machine, a "get-to-the-point" button.

—ALICIA BRANDT

Apartments

The walls of my apartment are so thin that when my neighbors have sex, I have an orgasm.

—LINDA HERSKOVIC

I live in your standard no-frills apartment. Just the basics: water, electricity, and more roaches than I'll ever be able to kill in a lifetime. Not that I've been able to kill any. I've had so many of them check out of the Roach Motel, I've had to hire a night clerk to help them with the luggage.

—ANDI RHOADS

Appliances

When I was young I used to lean up against the washer during the spin cycle to get a thrill. Now I just back up to the dryer to get warm.

—KATHIE DICE

On receiving a SaladShooter: What was I supposed to do? Walk into a bar and hold up a vegetarian?

—CAROL HENRY

Art

I'm taking an art class and the nude model just quit. Because I like to finger-paint.

—WENDY LIEBMAN

Artificial Insemination

Artificial insemination. That's a scary concept. You know why? I don't want to have coffee with a stranger, never mind have their child.

—ROSIE O'DONNELL

I prefer the old-fashioned way of having children. By accident.

—PHYLLIS DILLER

My husband and I tried really hard to have a baby, including having sex. But nothing happened. So we went to one of those fertility clinics where they charge you twelve million dollars every time your husband jerks off into a jar, but he was too uncomfortable there. Finally, to get a sample I had to fly him back home to his old room in his mother's house.

—KAREN HABER

Asses

I love looking at a man's tight tush. Which makes me wonder if Michelangelo's David took spinning classes.

—BONNIE CHEESEMAN

I like nothing more in the world than sitting on my ass doing nothing. And it's not my fault I have this attitude, because I happen to have an amazingly comfortable ass. It may not look like much, but if you could sit on this baby for two minutes, you'd realize that getting off this ass would be a crime against nature. I'm fighting the will of God every time I step on a StairMaster, and that's an uphill battle, let me tell you.

—LORI CHAPMAN

Astrology

I was talking to this friend and said, "I've been feeling really spaced out." And she said, "Mercury is in retrograde." Oh, that's the problem. It couldn't be all that pot I smoked.

—SABRINA MATTHEWS

Attitude

I think it's really important to maintain a positive attitude. It might not solve all your problems, but keep it up long enough and it will piss off enough people to make it worthwhile.

—MARGOT BLACK

I read a self-help book about a woman who cured her malignant liver tumor with positive thinking. I don't have enough happy thoughts to get rid of a zit.

—JANET ROSEN

Black women, we have attitude. We're the only people on earth born knowing how to roll our eyes with them closed.

—MARSHA WARFIELD

No matter how cynical you get, it's impossible to keep up.

—LILY TOMLIN

The chip on my shoulder's a little heavy. I have back problems now.

—JANEANE GAROFALO

I don't have pet peeves like some people. I have whole kennels of irritation.

—WHOOPI GOLDBERG

Sometimes I really hate myself. But I feel better when I hang out with like-minded people. So instead of me, I can hate them.

—SARI KARPLUS

Babies

I still can't believe that people I know, my peers, are making babies. I'm too lazy to make a salad.

—HELLURA LYLE

It's a good thing men can't have a baby. If they can't drive it, drink it, or display it, they won't take care of it.

—DIANA JORDAN

I can't decide if I want a baby. And my friends who have kids don't make very good salesmen. They're like, "Oh, you learn all this great stuff, like how to survive on two hours' sleep." If I want to learn that I'll just become a political prisoner or something.

—CATHRYN MICHON

For about a month after my baby was born I bragged to everyone that I had the perfect baby because he never cried. Then I realized those baby monitors have volume control.

—FRANCES DILORINZO

There's a lot to do when you have a baby. The first thing, which is taking me a really long time, I have to figure out who the father is.

—HEIDI JOYCE

I'm a new mother of two, and no, they're not twins. There's a medical term for a mother who gives birth to two babies within two years: suicidal.

—SUNDA CROONQUIST

I was asking my friend who has children, "What if I have a baby and I dedicate my life to it and it grows up to hate me. And it blames everything wrong with its life on me." And she said, "What do you mean, 'if'?"

—RITA RUDNER

I envy the kangaroo. That pouch setup is extraordinary; the baby crawls out of the womb when it is about two inches long, gets into the pouch, and proceeds to mature. I'd have a baby if it would develop in my handbag.

—RITA RUDNER

In my day there was no pill, it was trick or treat. I had far too many kids. At one time in our playpen it was standing-room only. It looked like a bus stop for midgets. It used to be so damp in there we had a rainbow above it.

—PHYLLIS DILLER

My sister is pregnant with her fifth baby, and had the nerve to tell me she's registered at Babies "R" Us. No way, I'm drawing the line! Where's my gift for *not* getting knocked up? I made it my whole life so far without getting pregnant once. And that's a real accomplishment, because I'm a slut.

—SHELLEY BRIGMAN

Women forty-nine years old are having their first child. Forty-nine! I couldn't think of a better way to spend my golden years. What's the advantage of having a kid at forty-nine? So you can both be in diapers at the same time?

—SUE KOLINSKY

Babies—no. Babies are just coasting on their youth and their looks. As a mother I'd be, "You're so young and cute. Now go get a job."

—JANET ROSEN

I'll never have a baby because I'm afraid I'll leave it on top of my car.

—LIZZ WINSTEAD

Baby Shower

My best friend is Lutheran and she told me that wh[en]
the Three Wise Men came to visit and brought frank[...
Myrrh? To a baby shower? I guess Mary was very polite about it, "Oh,
myrrh, how lovely. One can never get enough myrrh . . ."

—CATHY LADMAN

Baby-sitting

I baby-sit for my best friend's three-year-old. Don't kids say the darndest
things? When they're drunk?

—WENDY LIEBMAN

We used to terrorize our baby-sitters when I was little, except for my
grandfather because he used to read to us from his will.

—JANINE DITULLIO

Bachelorette Parties

I was at this club, full of a rowdy bachelorette party. The bride was so
drunk her veil was hanging in her margarita. It was disgusting, I finally said,
"Ma'am, as many times as I've been married, I've never gone out and gotten
drunk the night before the wedding. I always thought about the baby."

—VICKI BARBOLAK

I threw my best friend a bachelorette party. I could say I did this for her
last night of freedom. But frankly, after a year of fielding important bride
crises like, "Jordan almonds, or white chocolate–covered cashews?"
I've earned three pitchers of margaritas and a naked blue-collar worker.

—KELLY MAGUIRE

...ldness

Bald men. They get older and gravity starts sucking their hair back into their scalp, and shooting it out their ears.

—MARYELLEN HOOPER

I prefer balding men. Why would you want to run your hands through a man's hair, when you could shove your fist right into his skull?

—STEPHANIE HODGE

My husband is losing his hair, but I think bald is sexy. Michael Jordan, Yul Brenner, Bruce Willis, Homer Simpson: sexy. But guys, forget the half-hair, half-skin thing and trying to comb the hair on one side over the bald spot. Have some guts, have some confidence: Shave it all off. And hope to heaven you don't find a 666 birthmark your mother never told you about.

—LAURIE MCDERMOTT

Banking

At the ATM they ask if you'd like to conduct your business in English or Spanish. I suggest you try Spanish, because your account balance will look much better in pesos.

—TERE JOYCE

My bank bends over backwards not to help me. But how can I possibly get tough with them? "Look pal, I'll take my fourteen dollars right out of here and put it in the coffee can under my bed."

—JANEANE GAROFALO

I don't even have a savings account because I don't know my mom's maiden name, and apparently that's the key to the whole thing.

—PAULA POUNDSTONE

Bars

Generally not a good idea, meeting guys in a bar. It's like going grocery shopping when you're hungry; you bring home stuff you don't need.

—CORY KAHANEY

To me, guys in bars are all the same, white collar, blue collar, flea collar. They all just sniff around, scratch, and then look for a place to bury their bone.

—PAMELA YAGER

Guys should know that they're having a bad night in the bar when we break out the fake names. I'm not even discreet about it, "I'm Marsha, this is Jan, and that's Cindy. Our friend Alice is in the bathroom."

—CHRISTINA WALKINSHAW

I've actually seen a man walk up to four women sitting in a bar and say, "Hey, what are you doing all alone?"

—LILY TOMLIN

Bathing Suits

It's my least favorite season of the year, bathing-suit season. I don't know why we all can't be shaped like those eighteen-year-old boys they design those suits for.

—DIANE FORD

Guys' bathing suits haven't changed too much through the years. Either tight trunks or loose trunks, or those disgusting bikini things that make you want to lose your lunch. If I want to see a behind like that I'll have someone over to fix my refrigerator.

—DIANE FORD

I tried on this bathing suit and I looked like an upside-down map of Idaho. The blue veins were the interstates.

—KATE CLINTON

Men have an easier time buying bathing suits. Women have two types: depressing and more depressing. Men have two types: nerdy and not nerdy.

—RITA RUDNER

Bathrooms

Some of the bathrooms are fancy, they have railings on each side of the toilet, and you might assume that's for the elderly or handicapped. It's really for people who are paranoid about catching germs, they can balance themselves above the toilet. That iron cross is hard to do, I'll tell you that. And the dismount! You need a spotter, you do. That's why women go in pairs, "I'm going. Spot me." And when you do an incredible job the judges (you bet there are judges in there) yell, "*Ten!*"

—ELLEN DEGENERES

All I have to say about men and bathrooms is: they're not too specific.

—RITA RUDNER

Beauty Pageants

They tell us the Miss America pageant is a scholarship contest, not a beauty contest. If this were true, they'd go to Mensa for contestants. "Madeleine Albright, you passed the intelligence test to be Miss America. Now slip your ass into this swimsuit so we can see how smart you really are."

—JENNIFER VALLY

The Miss America pageant is very pro-education. They give the winner a full college scholarship. Which is just what Harvard needs, more bulimics who play the ukulele.

—SHEILA WENZ

I can't believe we still have the Miss America pageant. This is America! Where we're not supposed to judge people based on how they look; we're supposed to judge people based on how much money they make.

—HEIDI JOYCE

Bible

Even if you don't believe a word of the Bible, you've got to respect the person who typed all that.

—LOTUS WEINSTOCK

I was flipping through the Bible and saw that the meek will inherit the earth. Boy, is that going to be a long line. But a polite one; there'll be no cutting: "Oh, sorry, you're ahead of me." "No, no, you were here first." God might want to rethink that one.

—KATHLEEN KANZ

I'm Catholic and we don't read the Bible, we pay a priest to do that for us. Man's got all the week off and no wife. He can give us a forty-five-minute book report once a week. "Just weed through the crap and get to the plot, Padre."

—KATHLEEN MADIGAN

The Bible contains six admonishments to homosexuals, and 362 to heterosexuals. This doesn't mean God doesn't love heterosexuals; it's just that they need more supervision.

—LYNN LAVNER

Bills

I divide my bills into three categories: late bills; late, late bills; and "Would you buy my kidney?" bills.

—MARGOT BLACK

Biological Clock

I'm at the point where I have to decide if I'm going to have a baby or not. I have like twenty minutes. At my age, it's not a biological clock, it's an egg timer.

—JANET ROSEN

My biological clock isn't just ticking, the alarm's going off and I can't find the snooze button.

—CHRISTINE O'ROURKE

The hands on my biological clock are giving me the finger.

—WENDY LIEBMAN

Birds

Some birds mate for life. There's no divorce in the aviary world, apparently. I think that's why they fly into windows, it's the only way out.

—ROBIN FAIRBANKS

I bought a bird feeder. It was expensive, but I figured in the long run it would save me money on cat food.

—LINDA HERSKOVIC

I was outside smoking a cigarette and a bird flew over and pooped in my hair. My friend said, "Maybe the bird was trying to send you the message that you should quit smoking." Oh, yeah? Then what message are birds sending when they poop on a statue? "Screw you, St. Francis. What have you done for us lately?" I don't think birds are saying anything with their guano. And if they were, it would probably be along the lines of, "Thanks for the bread crumbs, we're full."

—LORI CHAPMAN

Eagles mate while flying at 80 miles an hour. And when they start to drop, they don't stop until the act is completed. So it's not uncommon they both hit the ground and die. That's how committed they are. Boy, don't we feel like wimps for stopping to answer the phone? I don't know about you, but if I'm one of those two birds and we're getting close to the ground, I would seriously consider faking it.

—ELLEN DEGENERES

Birth

I had a baby. I said to my husband, "Honey, it's time," and my husband, a cautious man who usually doesn't rush, got from our house to the hospital in five minutes. Then he had to go back and get me.

—JEAN CARROLL

I think the husband should always be in the delivery room, along with the child's father.

—MAUREEN MURPHY

I have friends who take home movies of their kids being born. If you're going to show me movies of your kid, I don't want to see them being born, I want to see them being conceived.

—JOAN RIVERS

We'd ask my mother what she wanted for her birthday. Every year she'd say the same thing, "What do I want for my birthday? I want you kids to get along. All I want is peace in this house." Well, we saved a lot of money on gifts.

—JUDY GOLD

I had the worst birthday party ever when I was a child, because my parents hired a pony to give rides. These ponies are never in good health, but this one dropped dead. It just wasn't much fun after that. One kid would sit on him and the rest of us would drag him around in a circle.

—RITA RUDNER

Books

I honestly believe there is absolutely nothing like going to bed with a good book. Or a friend who's read one.

—PHYLLIS DILLER

If you read a lot of books, you're considered well-read. But if you watch a lot of TV, you're not considered well-viewed.

—LILY TOMLIN

Stephen King writes some scary books. He's coming out with the scariest book he ever wrote, *A Husband with a Mind of Its Own.* Don't get scared, ladies. It's just a fantasy; it will never happen.

—ROSEANNE BARR

Born

When I was born I was so surprised, I couldn't talk for a year and a half.

—GRACIE ALLEN

a, b, c

I was born in Harrisburg, Pennsylvania, near the nuclear power plant Three Mile Island, and conceived within three months of the accident. So if I drink too much and glow in the dark, it's not my fault.

—CHRISTINA IRENE

Boyfriends

I haven't had a boyfriend for like a hundred years, and I'm at that point where I could really use a guy on a Saturday for about six hours. You know what I mean? Because everything in my apartment is broken.

—KAREN BERGREEN

One of my boyfriends wanted me to mother him. So I spit on a hankie and wiped his face.

—JENNY JONES

I'm thirty-three and have my first serious boyfriend. I finally found someone who likes the camp-counselor look.

—WENDY WILKINS

Boyfriend. This is such a weird word. There's no good word about someone if you're not married. Even calling a guy you live with your boyfriend makes you sound eleven years old. Old man? If you're not living with Willie Nelson, that one doesn't work, either.

—ELAYNE BOOSLER

We were incompatible in a lot of ways. Like for example, I was a night person, and he didn't like me.

—WENDY LIEBMAN

I have a totally wonderful new boyfriend. He calls me Cutie, which is short for chronic urinary tract infection. For Valentine's Day, he gave me cranberry juice.

—CAROLINE RHEA

When you get back together with an old boyfriend, it's pathetic. It's like having a garage sale and buying your own stuff back.

—LAURA KIGHTLINGER

I'm in my thirties and I've never really had a boyfriend. The older I get the more I realize I'm going to turn out to be someone's second wife.

—WENDY WILKINS

I always chose the wrong men, so now I have an imaginary boyfriend. The problem is I can't count on him. If I need someone to lean on and choose him, I fall over.

—PENELOPE LOMBARD

I'd like to have a boyfriend in prison so I'd always know where he is.

—CARRIE SNOW

Bras

Bras don't make any sense: A,B,C,D. What is this, a grade system? And isn't it interesting, the smaller you are, the better the grade.

—LANG PARKER

I was shopping for a bra and the salesgirl said, "The French say that the perfect breast fits in a champagne glass." "Well, I'm an American. You got anything that comes in a beer mug?"

—MARGOT BLACK

I stuff my bra. So if you get to second base with me, you'll find that the bases are loaded.

—WENDY LIEBMAN

I have enormous breasts. You can't tell because I wear minimizer bras. This is a bra that actually makes you look two sizes smaller. Instead of pushing you up and out, it sticks some under your arms where no one will notice.

—HEIDI JOYCE

My favorite marketing gimmick, the Wonderbra. Doesn't your date notice that your chest feels like a stuffed animal? And what happens when you get home and take it off? It's called the Wonderbra because the guy is sitting there thinking, "I wonder where her boobs went?"

—REBECCA NELL

Breakfast

Always eat breakfast. Your first meal of the day is the most important. Why? Because if you don't down a bran muffin before you walk out the door and get hit by a truck, you'll be dead on an empty stomach.

—JUDY TENUTA

Breaking Up

I think it's healthy for some people to break up. And some people can break up so easily, it's like, "You left your socks in the living room again. That's it!" And then, for other people, it's like, "You left your socks in the living room, you don't have a job, you've emptied my bank account, you've slept with my sister . . . and if it happens again, that's *it.*"

—JUDY CARTER

If you want to get rid of a man, I suggest saying, "I love you. I want to marry you. I want to have your children." Sometimes they leave skid marks.

—RITA RUDNER

My boyfriend dumped me. Or rather, I allowed him to set me free.

—DARLENE HUNT

I just dumped my boyfriend. I found some chick's stilettos under his bed. I won't date a man who has a time-share in his pants.

—ELAINE PELINO

I was going with someone for a few years but we broke up. It was one of those things. He wanted to get married, and I didn't want him to.

—RITA RUDNER

You want to know what the biggest kick in the pants is? When someone breaks up with you and starts dating someone fatter. *What?* Dude, I would've had the extra cheese.

—WENDY WILKINS

How do you like these slug puppets who break up with you and then date some clone who looks just like you except she's donated her brain to shopping.

—JUDY TENUTA

One and a half years into my marriage my husband ran off with a short, fat, squat-bodied, droopy-titted, bleached-blonde slut bimbo named Melissa. If you meet her, bring her to me, so I can thank her.

—MONIQUE MARVEZ

How many people still have that relationship with their ex, where you call each other up just to yell? It's like you're married: you're not having sex, and you're fighting.

—ROSIE TRAN

I have an ex-boyfriend who wants to stay a friend. That means he wants to keep in touch and tell me how miserable I am without him. He wrote me a letter, "I'm now seeing someone smarter and more successful than you." I responded, "I'm now seeing someone older and balder than you." That'll show him.

—MAURA LAKE

It's terrible when people break up with you, because they always say the same thing, "Let's still be friends." That's like being freed from a kidnapper and saying, "Keep in touch! Remember the torture? You call me."

—CAROLINE RHEA

My ex-boyfriend's mother told me that I hate men. I said, "I don't hate all men, just your son. That's just one guy."

—LAURA KIGHTLINGER

I think my neighbor broke up with his girlfriend last night, because he played "Ain't No Sunshine When She's Gone," thirteen times in a row.

—WENDY WILKINS

The hardest thing about getting out of a relationship is listening to the radio. Because every song is about being in love, or being heartbroken. And I found that the only song I was comfortable with is that Peter, Paul, and Mary song "If I Had a Hammer."

—ELLEN DEGENERES

The thing about breaking up when you get older, you just don't have the steam anymore. "Oh, that's it. I can't start shaving my legs above the knee again."

—ELAYNE BOOSLER

After a breakup, I'll date anyone. If a one-legged troll who lives under a bridge glances at me twice, it's Mardi Gras!

—KRIS MCGAHA

I spotted my ex-boyfriend at the mall. We had a really bad breakup, and I didn't want to make eye contact with him. Thank God I've had years of waitress training.

—KATE MASON

Breast-feeding

If I ever have a kid I'm definitely going to breast-feed it, because I don't know how to cook. I would be breast-feeding him through college. His friends will be jealous.

—WENDY LIEBMAN

Women breast-feeding in public always defend themselves by saying, "It's a beautiful thing." Yeah, so is sex, but I've never done it in the middle of Denny's. Although that at least would be a Grand Slam breakfast.

—TRACI SKENE

I'm not going to breast-feed. I've put this off so long, I'm sure my milk has expired.

—RITA RUDNER

Breast Implants

I actually thought about getting breast implants because I'm a radical militant feminist, and a hypocrite.

—MARIA BAMFORD

A boob job is the gift that keeps on giving. My ex bought them and my new guy enjoys them.

—ELAINE PELINO

This one girl I saw in *Playboy* was so amazing. I don't think she had silicone, I think she had helium. She was so big I couldn't keep the magazine closed.

—RITA RUDNER

I don't think women with implants are insecure about having small breasts, I think they just hate seeing their feet.

—JENNIFER POST

The women who got implants sued Dow Corning because they felt betrayed by their implant company. Betrayed? What, you mean I can't put a petroleum by-product in a Baggie and insert it in my chest cavity safely? I am shocked! And betrayed!

—DANI KLEIN

I've been thinking about getting breast implants. But if I get them, I want people to know I spent the money, so I'm thinking of getting four. Two up, two down. Now that's fancy.

—CATHRYN MICHON

Breasts

A lot of guys think the larger a woman's breasts are, the less intelligent she is. I think it's the opposite. I think the larger a woman's breasts are, the less intelligent the men become.

—ANITA WISE

My breasts still look pretty good because I wear a Wonderbra. Which makes my breasts wonder, "How did we get up here? This isn't our usual resting place, but what a great view!"

—SHEILA KAY

I nicknamed my boobs Thelma and Louise because every time I take off my bra, they look like they're trying to jump off a cliff and commit suicide.

—MEL FINE

Japanese women inherit their breasts from their fathers.

—TAMAYO OTSUKI

Bridal Showers

When my sister got married I threw her a bridal shower. What a nifty way to spend a Sunday afternoon, right, ladies? My aunt bought my sister a spice rack and thought it would be a nice idea to individually wrap all the spices. So for forty-five minutes we were going, *"Ooooh, paprika!"*

—ROSIE O'DONNELL

What's a bridal shower if you're gay? It's the parade of gifts you'll never get because you're homosexual. "Come in and take a look at the blender, toaster, silverware you'll have to buy yourself." I hate that. I don't bring a gift anymore, I take one. I have six Cuisinarts. I don't give a shit, they owe us.

—SUZANNE WESTENHOEFER

Bridesmaids

I hate the saying "Always a bridesmaid, never a bride." I like to put it into perspective by thinking, "Always a pallbearer, never a corpse."

—LAURA KIGHTLINGER

I hate being a bridesmaid because I have to dress to the bride's taste. My best friend sent me this black-purple, floor-length dress, two sizes too small. I shuffled down the aisle like the bridesmaid of Frankenstein. Just wait until I get married. Lucky Charms are my favorite cereal, and you're going as a leprechaun bridesmaid, bitch.

—TAMARA CASTLE

There are all kinds of magazines for brides, but I think they should have a *Bridesmaid* magazine, with helpful articles like, "Should You Get Drunk and Sleep with the Best Man at the Rehearsal Dinner, or Wait Until After the Ceremony?"

—KELLY MAGUIRE

Broke

You know you're poor when you envy people with bus passes.

—BONNIE MCFARLANE

My finances are so jacked up I'm on the cover of *Mis-Fortune*. Really, my credit is so bad I need a cosigner to play Monopoly.

—JOANNA BRILEY

I'm so broke I'm actually considering getting a second boyfriend.

—CHRISTINA WALKINSHAW

Brothers

I should understand men better than I do, because I grew up with brothers. I wanted sisters; they're better for a girl. They teach you how to put on makeup, how to do your hair, give you dating tips. You know what brothers teach you? How to unhook a bra with your teeth.

—CAROL SISKIND

Budget

I've been budgeting recently. I'm putting aside half of my paycheck each month for coffee and cigarettes. I know I shouldn't complain, but if you buy yourself a pack of cigarettes and throw in a latte from Starbucks, that's the equivalent of round-trip airfare.

—CINDEE WEISS

Cancer

I've been in remission from breast cancer for three years, and the hardest part was losing my breast. Now when I really want something, I can't say, "I'd give my left tit for that."

—LIZ SELLS

Candy

My parents used to stuff me with candy when I was a kid. M&M's, Jujubes, SweeTARTS. I don't think they wanted a child, I think they wanted a piñata.

—WENDY LIEBMAN

Career Counseling

Just saw a career counselor. Turns out I'd be perfect working for the airlines because I'm always late and I lose things.

—SIMONE ALEXANDER

Cars

I hate to valet park my '89 Mazda hunk-a-junk car because I'm paying ten dollars to explain how to drive the thing. "You have to start it in neutral. Don't lock it! Thank you, now I have to climb through the hatch."

—JACKIE KASHIAN

My car is so screwed up I'm hoping that AAA has a 12-step program for autos that can't hold their high test. I'm tired of finding it conked out under some bridge.

—CYNDI STILES

I drove a '65 Mustang. It was a great car, but it broke down all the time. I figured someday it was going to break down and I'd break down. They'd find me on the side of the road yelling at it like I was its parent. "Do you have any idea of how much money I've put into you this month alone? I give and give and give. Could you maybe take me two or three miles. Oh no. Look at all the cars. They are moving. You had to have new brake shoes. I buy them for you. You don't wear them."

—PAULA POUNDSTONE

My brother gave me his Pinto, but he neglected to tell me one thing: It doesn't handle well on pavement.

—CHRISTINE CROSBY

I hate cars. I hate driving them, putting gas in them, cleaning them, and wrecking them. But in all my years of driving I have learned several things:
1. No matter what your brother says, gasoline doesn't taste good.

2. E means "*empty*," not "*almost* empty." If it meant "almost empty" there would be an "A" there.

3. If you knock a car out of gear, it will roll down the hill either into a pond or into a neighbor's mailbox, fence, or the neighbor, if he doesn't get out of the way.

4. If you see a car take out your mailbox, and then your fence, get the heck out of the way.

5. Cops like to give out tickets.

—SANDI SELVI

My sister bought a new car with a global positioning device, so she never gets lost. Unfortunately, it's the Republican model and it won't let her turn left.

—DARYL HOGUE

My husband and I were shopping for a new car, and the salesman asked us if we'd consider leasing. He said, "Leasing is just like owning a car. You make the same monthly payments, but at the end of two years you turn the car in and get a new one." I asked my husband, "Baby, didn't we do that already?" and he replied, "No, sweetheart. *That* was a repossession."

—JODI BORRELLO

I was on my way to work the other day and I guess I got too close to someone's car, because the alarm started going off. I didn't want them to come back and be confused as to why it was going off, so I threw a brick through the windshield. I figured that would explain it.

—JESSICA DELFINO

I hate those new sport-utility vehicles. I just got cut off by that new one, you know, the Ford Exhibitionist.

—DARYL HOGUE

There is truth in what they say about the sexes. Men like cars, women likes clothes. I also like cars because they take me to clothes.

—RITA RUDNER

My boyfriend, like a lot of men, takes great pride in his car. Honey, his car is detailed, waxed, and vacuumed weekly. On the other hand, my car looks like a really big purse.

—DIANE NICHOLS

They say that the car a man drives is an extension of his penis. Is that why so many men drive small, fast cars? You'd think they'd want to impress people by driving a 1968 Buick LeSabre, missing a cylinder. Big and slow.

—JENNIFER VALLY

I've never known a man who wasn't deeply attached on a very emotional level to his beloved vehicle. Whether it was a piece of junk or a masterpiece made no difference. They rode in their metal boxes and were in control of their lives. I think I know why so many men are afraid to make a commitment to women. It's because we can't be steered.

—RITA RUDNER

Cats

I don't see the purpose of cats. Dogs can protect you, can sniff out things, and can be your eyes if you're blind. Could you imagine a Seeing Eye cat? The first person who walks by with an untied shoelace, and you're history.

—CHRISTINE O'ROURKE

I have a cat at home. She's an indoor cat. She's never been outside. She has no idea that there's even an outdoors. She thinks that when I leave for the day, I'm just standing on the other side of the door for twelve hours.

—TIG

My cats have fleas, which makes me feel bad because I live in a one-bedroom apartment, and they never go out. So if they got fleas, they got them from me. I feel like an ass for making them wear the collars.

—PAULA POUNDSTONE

I was out of town and my friend Nicki stayed at my apartment to watch my cat. When I got back, I saw that my cat had peed in my bed three times. Unless, of course, it's Nicki who is mad at me.

—CHRISTINE BLACKBURN

I found out why cats drink out of the toilet. My mother told me, it's because it's cold in there. And I'm like, "How did my mother know that?"

—WENDY LIEBMAN

My cat is depressed. I had the exterminators in and they killed all his toys.

—ANITA WISE

Ever put a vacuum on the cat? They will not always come when called, and you can use that suction as a unique teaching device.

—PAULA POUNDSTONE

I have a boyfriend and four male cats, so basically I have five male cats. They all demand to be fed the moment I set foot in the house, followed by heavy petting.

—ANDI RHOADS

The problem with cats is that they get the same exact look whether they see a moth or an ax-murderer.

—PAULA POUNDSTONE

My cat is fourteen and for the first time, I gave him catnip. He's got diabetes, arthritis, and kidney trouble, so I figured it would be like medical marijuana for him. And he loved it. Gobbled that catnip up and meowed for more. But I think I may have given Kitty too much catnip, because he's now on tour with Phish.

—WENDY WILKINS

Celebrities

We should pass a new law: Nobody can get famous just by sleeping with a celebrity and getting naked in a magazine. You have to make a contribution to society first. You can still be in *Playboy*, you just have to do something worthwhile beforehand. "I developed a vaccine, and I'd like to show you my breasts." Go ahead, you've earned it.

—ELAYNE BOOSLER

Larry Flynt is now spokesman for organ donation. How novel of him to be hocking his own body parts for a change.

—BETSY SALKIND

A British documentary on Michael Jackson said he's only had two plastic surgeries. Both were on his nose. One was to remove it, and the other was to glue it back on.

—CAROLINE RHEA

Martha Stewart. If there's anything at all to reincarnation, that bitch will come back as a Brillo pad.

—PHYLLIS DILLER

That Anna Nicole slut. We should suck the fat from her breasts and make them shelters for the homeless.

—JUDY TENUTA

At eighty-eight, the king of popcorn, Orville Redenbacher, passed away. His family is mired in an ugly dispute over whether to cremate, microwave, or air pop him.

—STEPHANIE MILLER

Celibacy

I'm celibate, and it ain't easy. I now know why Catholic nuns are so darn mean. I also want to hit people with a ruler for no apparent reason.

—RENÉ HICKS

CEOs

These CEOs are scary; they affected the rest of people's lives. Now when I walk past a gangbanger I don't even blink but if I see a white dude with a *Wall Street Journal,* I haul ass. Before I walk past the Arthur Andersen building, I'll cut through the projects. I might lose what I have on me that day, but I ain't never been mugged of my future.

—WANDA SYKES

Cheap

My father was so cheap. When my parents were engaged, he didn't give my mother a diamond ring. He gave her a lump of coal and told her to be patient.

—CATHY LADMAN

When a date is cheap with me I like to blame J. Lo. All her songs talk about how low-maintenance she is: "My Love Don't Cost a Thing," "I'm Real," and of course, my favorite, "I'm So Cheap, I'll Pay You."

—MAURA LAKE

Cheerleading

When I was growing up in Oklahoma, I wanted to be a cheerleader, but I never made the squad. I thought it was because I couldn't do a back handspring. I later found out it was because I wasn't pregnant.

—SHAWN PELOFSKY

I went to an all-girls school. I was captain of the virginity team. "Go, go, go. No, no, no."

—CAROLINE RHEA

Childhood

Do you ever remember having a bad hair day when you were five? Hell, no. You're five years old, you wake up in the morning, your hair's standing straight on end, "I look good! I been sleepin' in my bathing suit and I feel fine!" You do that when you were a kid, sleep in your bathing suit? Oh man, I wouldn't even take it off to go to the bathroom. I just moved it on over.

—ELVIRA KURT

A lot of things go on when you're a kid that you don't figure out until you're an adult. Like, I think my kindergarten teacher had a drinking problem, because nap time was every day from nine o'clock to two-thirty.

—JANINE DITULLIO

I miss being a kid. I got food, clothing, and shelter for free. Grown-ups only get that in jail.

—LEIGHANN LORD

Being from a family of immigrants can be frustrating and embarrassing. You get fucked-up shit in your lunch box. All the other kids would get granola bars and Capri Sun in their lunch, and I'd get dried fish. All the other kids got Ho Hos and Ding Dongs, I would get squid and peanuts. You can't trade that.

—MARGARET CHO

My childhood was kind of a blur, to tell you the truth. I needed better glasses.

—WENDY LIEBMAN

Growing up was rough. Most of the responsibility for my ever-growing family was up to me. Joyce would not leave my side, Carl had eye problems, Betsy lost a leg. Finally I said, "I cannot raise any more stuffed animals; I have no time to myself." Eventually they all left home to join the Salvation Army.

—WENDY SPERO

My childhood was pretty bad. When I was seven, my mother told me I was selfish. One day I asked for dinner. "You're just like your father," she said.

—GLORIA BRINKWORTH

As a child I experienced a lot of betrayal. One time I ran into my baby-sitter, and she was with another kid. They were holding hands and the kid wasn't even cute. And I recently found out my baby-sitter was only with me for the money.

—WENDY SPERO

Child Support

Somewhere over the rainbow, the child support check is in the mail.

—JULIE KIDD

When I turned eighteen, my mother sent me to my father to get my child support check. My father gave me this lecture, "Money, money, money, that's all she wants. You don't believe me? Tell your mother this is the last check she's going to get, and watch the expression on her face." So I told my mother what my father had said. Without missing a beat she said, "Oh really? Go back and tell Tommy I said he ain't your father, and watch the expression on his face!"

—LYDIA NICOLE

Circumcision

I went to my nephew's bris. That's where a little Jewish baby boy is circumcised, and all the friends and family get together. What a festive event! I think this is rather inappropriate. I wouldn't invite you to my internal exam, "Happy pap smear!" "Have some nachos, I passed my test."

—CATHY LADMAN

My son was circumcised by his father, who's not a doctor, just cheap.

—DARYL HOGUE

Clichés

Clichés confuse me, like: "That which does not kill me makes me stronger." Are you saying that a set of weights is going to fall on me? Because, yeah, lifting that off would certainly build some muscle.

—KATHLEEN KANZ

Whoever came up with the saying "Don't bite the hand that feeds you" definitely owned a cat.

—CHRISTINE O'ROURKE

I don't think there's any such a thing as a cash cow. If there were, I'd take a baseball bat and bash it like it was a piñata.

—CYNDI STILES

My mom always says, "Keep your chin up." That's how I ran into the door.

—DARYL HOGUE

I've heard that dogs are man's best friend. That explains where men are getting their hygiene tips.

—KELLY MAGUIRE

Why do today what you can put off till tomorrow?

—JANEANE GAROFALO

Just when I think that I have it down, I find I'm actually trapped underneath it.

—KATHLEEN KANZ

Benjamin Franklin was wrong. In my experience, "Early to bed, and early to rise," makes a man dull, anal, and horny.

—GLORIA BRINKWORTH

Every time I try to find myself I'm in the last place I looked.

—MARGOT BLACK

Thomas Wolfe wrote, "You can't go home again." You can, but you'll get treated like an eight-year-old.

—DARYL HOGUE

She who laughs last didn't get the joke quickly enough.

—RITA RUDNER

I decided to go visit the pet cemetery where my dead dog Buster was buried. My grandmother always used to say, "When life gives you lemons, make lemonade." But you can't make lemonade out of a dead dog, no matter how hard you try.

—JULIE BROWN

Life isn't fair. If it were, my running shoes would keep me running right past all those doughnut shops.

—JOHNNYE JONES GIBSON

People say, "There's a light at the end of the tunnel." Yeah, it's a train.

—MARGARET SMITH

They say, "Suffering builds character." I disagree. Suffering doesn't build character, it turns you into one. I don't care how much character I have, if I'm standing in traffic wearing a stained housecoat and yelling at cars, I'd rather be shallow.

—KATHLEEN KANZ

If truth is beauty, how come no one has their hair done in a library?

—LILY TOMLIN

It's an ill wind that blows when you leave the hairdresser.

—PHYLLIS DILLER

The world is my oyster. Too bad it smells like fish.

—KATHLEEN KANZ

Things are going to get a lot worse before they get worse.

—LILY TOMLIN

Clitorectomy

There are countries in the world where it's the custom for the men there to cut off a woman's clitoris. This is true and very gruesome. We should be happy that this will never happen in our country, because the men here don't know where the clitoris is.

—JANINE DITULLIO

Cloning

"Human cloning would not lead to identical souls, because only God can create a soul," a panel set up by Pope John Paul has concluded. They also took care of a couple other things that were burning issues: Apparently, Trix are indeed for kids.

—JANEANE GAROFALO

Clothing

When I'm not working I like to be comfortable and so I wear what most people would call "laundry clothes." Clothes that are washed, torn, and pulled to an inch of their life. I have a pair of crotchless underwear that I like to wear. They weren't made that way, they're just that old.

—WENDY WILKINS

Exercise fosters unhealthy ideas about small, clingy shirts and low-slung jeans. Constricting clothing limits oxygen flow to the brain, thereby reducing personality capacity among the physically fit. The sins of pride are usually located near the StairMaster. So stay pure and sit down.

—JANEANE GAROFALO

I'm having a problem with these low-waisted pants. Who are these pants designed for? Teenage Vietnamese boys? I'm afraid if I drop my keys, I'll look like a plumber.

—CORY KAHANEY

When a woman tries on clothing from her closet that feels tight, she will assume she has gained weight. When a man tries on clothing from his closet that feels tight, he will assume the clothing has shrunk.

—RITA RUDNER

The clothes I'm wearing are too tight. I recently lost weight, and I'm whoring it up too soon.

—JACKIE KASHIAN

Women know the weight of every item of clothing they own, so we don't have to get on the scale naked. We just deduct. For instance, I know my sweats weigh in at exactly twenty-one pounds.

—CHRISTINA IRENE

I'm reading *Hints from Heloise,* and she says that if you put an angora sweater in the freezer for an hour, it won't shed for the rest of the day. And I'm thinking, "My cat sheds an awful lot."

—ELLEN DEGENERES

Codependence

I'm actually writing my own book on codependence. So far all I have is a title, "Hey, I Was Just Trying to Be Nice"

—KATE CLINTON

I'm not codependent myself, but aren't they great to have around?

—BETSY SALKIND

Coffee

Studies show that women who drink three cups of coffee or more each day are less likely to commit suicide. Well, yeah, who could hold a gun steady?

—MARGOT BLACK

You can tell a lot about someone's personality by how he orders coffee. "Decaf, please, skim milk, no sugar." That's the kind of a guy who goes through the car wash wearing a seat belt.

—MARGOT BLACK

Coffeehouses

They just opened a new Starbucks, in my living room.

—JANEANE GAROFALO

Starbucks doesn't have a slogan yet, so I've thought of one for them: "It's really expensive, but the line is long!"

—KAREN BERGREEN

People are going on dates now to coffee bars. This is the worst idea. Four cappuccinos later, your date doesn't look any better.

—MARGOT BLACK

College

I went to college because they told me it was going to prepare me for the real world. Since when does the real world have spring break?

—LIVIA SQUIRES

I majored in animal husbandry in college, which is good, because I married a couple of pigs.

—SHEILA KAY

In college I majored in entomology, which is the study of Entenmann's baked goods. I had a crumb-cake concentration with a minor in maple walnut Häagen-Dazs. My undergrad thesis was entitled "How to Lose Fifteen Pounds in a Week and Gain It Back over Brunch." It was an essay on that obscure Arthur Miller play *A View from the Fridge*.

—WENDY KAMENOFF

I majored in nursing. I had to drop it. I ran out of milk.

—JUDY TENUTA

In college, everyone makes mistakes; mine was that I joined a sorority. Sororities are like cults, only less reading.

—DAVA KRAUSE

I went to this big party school, but I began to think I was going out too much when my weekends were starting on Tuesday night.

—MELANIE RENO

I went to the University of South Florida for five and a half years. Then I sobered up, got dressed, and went home—they still have my earrings.

—TRACY SMITH

I have a master's degree in psychology. I'm over forty, still single, no kids, with a cat, but now I know why.

—JILL TURNBOW

Cologne

What are men wearing? Why do they think women like horse saddles and pine sap? If a man wanted me to follow him down the street, he should wear something called "Butter Cookie" or, even better, "Croissant."

—RITA RUDNER

Communication

I personally think we developed language because of our deep inner need to complain.

—LILY TOMLIN

I have e-mail, a pager, a cell phone, a fax line. I've got an answering machine, three phone lines at home, one in my purse, and a phone in my car. The only excuse I have if I don't return your call is I just don't like you.

—ALICIA BRANDT

That movie *Fatal Attraction* really ruined things for women. I mean, you can't even call a guy a hundred and fifty times a day anymore without having them get all bent out of shape.

—LISA GOICH

Complaining

Complaining burns calories. That's why skinny women are always such bitches.

—DEBBIE KASPER

Computers

Computers are like dogs. They smell fear.

—SIMONE ALEXANDER

What do people mean when they say, "The computer went down on me?"

—MARILYN PITTMAN

I got a computer. I wrote an apology note to my VCR for ever thinking it was difficult. You find someone in this country who can print out an envelope. Maybe the fifth envelope, but you have to kill four to get to the fifth one.

—ELAYNE BOOSLER

I don't own a computer. I'm waiting for the kind where I can look at the screen and say, "Hey, I need a pizza," and one comes out and hits me in the eyebrows.

—KATHLEEN MADIGAN

Confidence

You get more confident when you're married. When you're single and you don't hear from your boyfriend, you wonder, "Should I call him?" When you're married and you don't hear from your husband, you wonder *what* you should call him.

—RITA RUDNER

Congress

We have the best congressmen that money can buy.

—JOANN DEARING

We've got fourteen women in the Senate. Fourteen women in the Senate? We are 52 percent of the population. Apparently women do suck at math.

—PAULA POUNDSTONE

Contraception

Japanese women are refusing to take birth control pills, opting to leave contraception up to men. Do you know what they call women who leave birth control up to men? Mothers.

—JENNIFER VALLY

You know what's the worst contraceptive? The pill. Because you have to keep taking it every day, regardless of what's going on in your love life. It's so nice during those two-year lulls to have a daily reminder. "I sleep alone, but oh my, look, it's time for my loser pill." Can you imagine if men had to wear a condom for thirty days just in case they might need it? "It's day twenty-eight, but somebody might call."

—CAROLINE RHEA

Other women take the pill and don't get pregnant. I take the pill and get a mustache and beard.

—ANDI RHOADS

I'm not on the pill, but I label my Tic Tacs with the days of the week. Makes me feel like I'm in a relationship.

—CATHY LADMAN

I'm getting off the pill because the hormones trick your body into thinking it's already pregnant. A lot of guys want to get their girlfriends on the pill so they can have unprotected sex. But I'm not sure making a girl feel bloated, stressed, and pissed off 24-7 is the best technique for having better sex, men. Unless you're turned on by crying jags, and like foreplay that includes watching her eating honey buns and pickles at the twenty-four-hour doughnut shop.

—ROSIE TRAN

I've got three kids. I had one with the birth control pill, one with a diaphragm, and another with the IUD. I don't know what happened to my IUD, but I have my suspicions. That kid picks up HBO.

—ROSEANNE BARR

The most effective birth control I know is a toddler with the croup and diaper rash.

—KATE ZANNONI

I was dating a control freak. He insisted that *he* take the birth control pills.

—WENDY LEIBMAN

I practice birth control, which is being around my sister's children. You want to run right out and ovulate after you play with them for five minutes.

—BRETT BUTLER

Read the condom boxes, they're pretty funny. Trojans say, "new shape." I didn't know this was necessary. Another box said, "reservoir." I said, "You mean these things can actually generate hydroelectric power?" I saw this new great brand: extra-supersensitive condoms. I thought, "Wow! These must hang around and talk to you after the guy leaves."

—ELAYNE BOOSLER

I was onstage last night talking. I said, "The diaphragm is a pain in the ass." Someone yelled out, "You were putting it in the wrong way."

—CAROL MONTGOMERY

The best contraceptive is the word *no* repeated frequently.

—MARGARET SMITH

I'm Catholic. My mother and I were unpacking and she found my diaphragm. I had to tell her it was a bathing cap for my cat.

—LIZZ WINSTEAD

Cooking

I've been so busy, I don't even have time to cook for my kids. I don't wanna say we eat out a lot, but I've noticed that lately when I call my kids for dinner they run to the car.

—JULIE KIDD

I'm learning to cook. I made a casserole. The only trouble is, when I wanted to take it out of the oven, I realized I don't own any oven mitts. But luckily, since I'm a big sports fan, I had two "number one!" foam hands. Which makes your casserole presentation oh, so much more dramatic.

—SUE MURPHY

I try to be nice. Whenever I take something out of the freezer I say, "Welcome to the future."

—MEG MALY

I can't cook. I use a smoke alarm as a timer.

—CAROL SISKIND

Every time I go near the stove, the dog howls.

—PHYLLIS DILLER

My husband says I feed him like he's a god; every meal is a burnt offering.

—RHONDA HANSOME

Men are very strange. When they wake up in the morning they want things like toast. I don't have these recipes.

—ELAYNE BOOSLER

Men like to barbecue. Men will cook if danger is involved.

—RITA RUDNER

A word of advice for women: Go with a guy who cooks. Trust me, I've dated extensively and had a few husbands, and I know what I'm talking about. If you teach a man to fish he'll fish all damn day. But marry a man who likes to cook fish and you've not only got poached salmon crepes for breakfast, but he also does the shopping.

—CHRISTINE BLACKBURN

I think Martha Stewart is freakin' hot. Everything she does on that show sounds so sexy: "Today we're making a lovely bundt cake, any flavor you *desire*. Watch as I *knead the dough with my strong, long fingers*. Here we have one *hot and fresh and steaming* from the oven, as I ladle the icing over the top and it *oozes* down the side."

—SUZANNE WESTENHOEFER

Cosmetics

Makeup is such a weird concept. I'll wake up in the morning and look in the mirror: "Gee, I really don't look so good. Maybe if my eyelids were blue, I'd be more attractive."

—CATHY LADMAN

I wear so much makeup you could stick a finger on my face and write, "Wash me." I know my makeup looks good when I can put a dipstick in it and get a reading.

—LEMAIRE

I use an eyebrow pencil to color in my eyebrows because I plucked all my eyebrows out when I was trying to make them even. Three hairs left above each eye, and then I color them in too high. Great, now I look shocked at everything I see.

—MARYELLEN HOOPER

I want to do my own makeup commercial: "My old lip color could barely keep up with my busy schedule. In the time it took to notice the wide discrepancy between my salary and that of my male peers, my lipstick would be as invisible as this glass ceiling above my head."

—MARIA BAMFORD

I can't stand makeup commercials. "Do you need a lipstick that keeps your lips kissable?" No, I need a lipstick that gets me equal pay for equal work. How about eye shadow that makes me stop thinking I'm too fat?

—HEIDI JOYCE

It's very hard to sleep in your eye makeup and not wake up looking like Petie from the *Little Rascals*.

—ELAYNE BOOSLER

I don't wear makeup because I was raised by the wolves. All male wolves. They didn't wear makeup. Although one did wear deodorant, so I learned about that. So that's good.

—ELLEN DEGENERES

I don't have time every day to put on makeup. I need that time to clean my rifle.

—HENRIETTE MANTEL

All men are afraid of eyelash curlers. I sleep with one under my pillow instead of a gun.

—RITA RUDNER

Crafts

Martha Stewart is crazier than a bedbug. Did you ever watch that show? "Today we're making a lovely cranberry wreath. Just pick three or four thousand cranberries, hand wash them individually, and buff each one to a high gloss." You're writing it down until you realize you won't live long enough, you'll be handing it down for generations, begging, "Somebody please finish the damn thing!"

—SUZANNE WESTENHOEFER

Credit Cards

My last credit card bill was so big, before I opened it I actually heard a drum roll.

—RITA RUDNER

I'm in a long-term relationship with Citibank Visa. They call me all the time. I think they just want me to feel loved.

—MARY GALLAGHER

I just had plastic surgery; they cut up all my credit cards. Except for my Discover card, which nobody takes.

—WENDY LIEBMAN

Crime

Ninety-eight percent of the adults in this country are decent, hard-working, honest Americans. It's the other 2 percent that get all the publicity. But, then, we elected them.

—LILY TOMLIN

I got my purse stolen, so naturally I felt I had to embellish on my insurance claim. "Yeah, I had a lot of money in there, some jewelry, a CD player, a pair of skis, and a silver goblet, fourteenth-century."

——JANEANE GAROFALO

Somebody broke the window of my hunk-a-junk car and stole my $100 Radio Shack tape deck. Hey, who locks an '89 Mazda? Check the door, and take what you want.

—JACKIE KASHIAN

They caught the first female serial killer in Florida. Eight men. But she didn't kill them. She gained access to their homes, hid the remote controls, so they killed themselves.

—ELAYNE BOOSLER

People in New York were being killed for their coats. I don't think that's right. If you are gonna kill someone for their coat, I think you should eat them too.

—LAURA KIGHTLINGER

"Crimes of passion," that phrase drives me crazy. A man murdering his girlfriend is not a crime of passion. Premature ejaculation, *that's* a crime of passion.

—HELLURA LYLE

Whenever a heinous crime is committed, a newscaster will say that the criminal felt no remorse. Well, what could they say? "Damn, I just cut up ten people and shoved them down the toilet. I'm such an idiot. I'm always doing shit like that. I suppose they're all dead now, right? Oh, I could kick myself."

—LAURA KIGHTLINGER

I envy serial killers. Not the killing part, I just wish I could be that focused.

—LEMAIRE

Men and women perceive crime differently. Once when I was walking in New York with a boyfriend, he said, "Gee, it's a beautiful night. Let's go down by the river." "What? Are you nuts?" I asked. "It's midnight! I'm wearing jewelry! I'm carrying money! I have a vagina with me! Tomorrow," I added, "I'll leave it in my other pants. Then we'll go down."

—ELAYNE BOOSLER

Cruises

We took a cruise. It depends on the boat. You have to get on a good boat. They have the Fantasy, the Ecstasy ... we were on the Hysterectomy.

—RITA RUDNER

Crying

Men do cry, but only when assembling furniture.

—RITA RUDNER

Cursing

We shouldn't curse with sexual words. It gives sex a bad name in a situation like that. And it doesn't make sense. You're driving, someone cuts you off on the road, almost kills you, you roll down the window, wish them the nicest possible thing in the world. We need new curses that really mean something, like, "Oh, yeah? Well, *audit* you, buddy!"

—ELAYNE BOOSLER

D, E, F

Dancing

My mom took up belly dancing. In order to make it appear like she was moving, my father and I had to jiggle the furniture in back of her.

—RITA RUDNER

Dating

I think women have it much easier than men on the first date. Because they still have to call us up. That means they like us, they called. Nobody ever calls you to say, "I won't be dating you."

—DIANE NICHOLS

My rules for dating: I don't want to hear about your car, I don't want to hear about your ex-girlfriend, I don't want to hear about your boring-ass job. The most romantic thing you can do is relax, buy me drinks, and shut the hell up.

—WANDA SYKES

First dates are always so awkward. I find myself thinking, "Is it too soon for a kiss? No, I can do this, why not? Oh my God, that's my tongue! Why are there suddenly tongues involved? Okay, I need to stop now, I need to slow down, this is getting too heated, too fast. Whatever happens, I need to keep my clothes on and my hands out of his pants, because it's too soon, and other people in the restaurant are trying to eat."

—LORI CHAPMAN

This guy asked me out to dinner, and at the end of the dinner he told me he didn't bring his wallet. I was pissed; the bill was $120. You'd better believe I made him put out. I brought him home, and he had the nerve to start taking his clothes off. "Oh no, fool, this isn't about you. I paid, this is my time, and you can start by doing the dishes."

—TINA KIM

My father always said, "Be the kind they marry, not the kind they date." So on our first date I'd nag the guy for a new dishwasher.

—KRIS MCGAHA

A friend of mine went on a blind date but when I asked her about it, she said she wasn't going to see the guy again because "He was nice. But *too* nice, if you know what I mean." No, I don't know what you mean. I never ended a date by saying, "You bought me dinner, you paid for a movie, the next thing I know, you're going to give me compliments and try to satisfy me in bed. Screw you, buddy, I'm not that kind of a girl! What do I have to do to hear a 'Shut up, bitch, and get me a beer'?"

—LORI CHAPMAN

I don't hang out in bars and I don't date online. So for me there's basically two ways to meet men and they both suck: blind dates, which are a disaster, or getting fixed up, which is just a blind date with witnesses.

—ROBIN ROBERTS

I thought it would be so easy to meet guys when I got out of college, because it was very easy to meet guys in college. This was really all you had to say to meet some guy then: "Ohmigod, I'm *so* wasted!"

—DINA PEARLMAN

Why is it whenever you go out to dinner with someone you'd really like to impress, you leave the bathroom with a little piece of toilet paper still stuck to your tongue?

—LAURA KIGHTLINGER

Going out with a jerky guy is kind of like having a piece of food caught in your teeth. All your friends notice it before you do.

—LIVIA SQUIRES

I met a guy in line at the post office. He said, "With a face like yours I feel like I can tell you anything." And he did. "I lost my last four jobs, they fired me, and my car got repossessed." So I gave him my phone number. He called and said, "I'm calling from the Laundromat, my phone has been shut off, and I'm running out of change, but I'd like to take you out. For a walk." I replied, "Oh, no, I don't do things like *that* on a first date."

—DEBBIE SUE GOODMAN

I've always wanted to date a man who travels. Dreams do come true; I'm now seeing a bus driver.

—JULIE KIDD

I've been on so many blind dates I should get a free dog.

—WENDY LIEBMAN

When I was younger I'd go out with men who lived with their mother. Now if I'm with a man who lives with his mother, her last name better be Streisand or Trump.

—SUNDA CROONQUIST

It's too much trouble to get laid. Because you have to go out with a guy, and go to dinner with him, and listen to him talk about his opinions, and I don't have that kind of time.

—KATHY GRIFFIN

Dating is dumb. Basically you're making false judgments based on false exteriors. Oh sure, my superficial self likes your superficial self, but the real me likes your roommate.

—MARGOT BLACK

They say they're going to call you at about seven o'clock. It's seven and they haven't called. So you say, okay, I'll fix myself a drink. So you have a drink, then you have another, then you have another, and you have another. Now you're drunk. It's five after seven and they still haven't called.

—ELLEN DEGENERES

Whenever I want a really nice meal, I start dating again.

—SUSAN HEALY

I dated an illegal alien for a while, but that was really inconvenient because wherever we went he rode in the trunk of my car.

—ROBIN ROBERTS

I was out on a date recently and the guy took me horseback riding. That was kind of fun, until we ran out of quarters.

—SUSIE LOUCKS

Dating in your twenties is like getting a science project: "What did you get? I got an alcoholic; I'm going to change him!"

—CAROLINE RHEA

I tell men, if you want to impress a woman don't send her flowers, send her a maid. Because if you spend fifty-five dollars on a dozen roses, they're dead the next day. A maid costs about forty dollars and you still have fifteen dollars left to get Chinese food and one rose. By the time you come over we haven't cleaned, and you have food, a rose, and you. Baby, we'll do you all night long.

—LUDA VIKA

I went out to dinner with a Marine. He looked across the table and he goes, "I could kill you in seven seconds." I go, "I'll just have toast then."

—MARGARET SMITH

I went out with this one guy. I was very excited about it. He took me out to dinner, he made me laugh, he made me pay. He's like, "Oh, I'm sorry. I forgot my wallet." "Really? I forgot my vagina."

—LISA SUNDSTEDT

How many of you ever started dating someone because you were too lazy to commit suicide?

—JUDY TENUTA

I'm still going on bad dates, when by now I should be in a bad marriage.

—LAURA KIGHTLINGER

My sister was with two men in one night. She could hardly walk after that. Can you imagine? Two dinners!

—SARAH SILVERMAN

When you're first single, you're so optimistic. At the beginning, you're like, "I want to meet a guy who's really smart, really sweet, really good-looking, has a really great career." Six months later, you're like, "Lord, any mammal with a day job."

—CAROL LEIFER

I have one pick-up line which never works. If I'm at a club and I see a guy I like, I smile and if he smiles back and I feel really comfortable I'll walk over and say, "Stick it in!"

—MARGARET CHO

I'm standing on line at the bakery, and this really cute guy asked for my number. So I had to get another one.

—WENDY LIEBMAN

If you got fixed up on a blind date by your very best friend, wouldn't you think that within the top ten descriptive adjectives, "lazy eye" would be mentioned? We went out for a while, but I found out he was seeing someone on the side.

—CAROLINE RHEA

Let's begin by discussing dinner dates. This concept of traditional courting bothers me. I don't want food interrupting my two grueling days of pre-date starvation.

—JANEANE GAROFALO

My favorite thing to do on a date is go to dinner. Or should I say, have somebody else pay for my food.

—REBECCA NELL

D. E. F

A man on a date wonders if he'll get lucky. The woman knows.

—MONICA PIPER

It's hard to meet someone new. But it's easy for this friend of mine because she has very low standards. Like, she'll go home with a guy just for the free T-shirt.

—JANN KARAM

I'm dating again, but it's got me confused. So I've been reading up on the differences between men and women. I read *The Rules,* the Mars and Venus books, *Dating for Dummies.* And here's the real difference: Women buy the books.

—DARYL HOGUE

Dinner is a waste on a first date, because you don't want the guy to see how much you can really eat. "He'll find out soon enough that I can put my entire head in a Häagen-Dazs tub."

—MARYELLEN HOOPER

I was dating a stunt man for a while, which is a lot like dating a regular guy. He picks me up, takes me out to dinner, but when he drops me off he doesn't stop the car.

—JENNIFER SIEGAL

Dating is like driving on the freeway; I can never get to where I'm supposed to be. I know I should be at the corner of "Engaged to be Married," but instead I'm stuck in the "Valley of Haven't Had an Orgasm for Three Months."

—CHRISTINE O'ROURKE

I once dated a guy who was so dumb he couldn't count to twenty-one unless he was naked.

—JOAN RIVERS

Single women, date a lot of guys before you get married. I had what I called my series of Time/Life boyfriends. I examined them for fourteen days, kept the ones I wanted, and hung on to the free gifts.

—TRACI SKENE

I'm a nice girl. I hate it on the first date when I accidentally have sex.

—EMMY GAY

After two years I said to my boyfriend, "Either tell me your name or it's over."

—RITA RUDNER

I got desperate and went to one of those expensive matchmakers. She was so romantic: "You've got to get a guy on the hook. You reel him in slowly." I asked, "When do I fillet him?" I don't know much more about relationships, but I can run a fish-and-chips.

—MAURA LAKE

I just read a new book about how to catch a man. I did pretty good, I've got three of them stuffed and mounted.

—MARGOT BLACK

I spend all my time on dates playing this little game called "I'm not shallow." Every guy is afraid of being taken. It's a real chore convincing them I'm sincere: "Go ahead, use the coupon. Let's watch the movie you own, not that expensive $3.25 rental. I like you for you, not those chest implants."

—MAURA LAKE

It's the end of your blind date/Internet date/dating service date. You say to him, "It was very nice meeting you, good luck!" Translation: Step aside, *next!*

—NANCY PATTERSON

After you've dated someone it should be legal to stamp them with what's wrong with them so the next person doesn't have to start from scratch.

—RITA RUDNER

My mother on *The Dating Game,* how great would that be? "Bachelor Number Two: We're at a dinner dance at the temple, I fall and break a hip, do you: A. Stay with me on the dance floor, B. Run and get help, C. Leave me there to *drop dead just like my kids would.*"

—JUDY GOLD

My grandmother's ninety. She's dating. He's ninety-three. They're very happy, they never argue. They can't hear each other.

—CATHY LADMAN

Daughters

My daughter was rubbing my legs, giving me a mommy massage. She said, "Mom, your skin is so soft." I thought, "Oh, how sweet." Then she said, "Soft like Play-Doh. I'm gonna make a dinosaur now, okay?"

—MEL FINE

I have an eighteen-year-old; her name is Alexis. I chose that name because if I hadn't had her, I'd be driving one.

—ROBIN FAIRBANKS

Death

These people with near-death experiences always say the same thing. "I remember seeing this really bright white light." Of course you did, pinhead, it's the paramedic looking in your pupils with a penlight.

—CAROL LEIFER

I thought my husband never would die . . . I shouldn't talk like that about him, though. He dead. They say you shouldn't say nothing about the dead unless you can say something good. He dead. Good.

—MOMS MABLEY

Dentists

I have the biggest crush on my dentist, he's so cute. I've been doing everything to see him, I've been gargling with Coke. But it's hard to flirt with your dentist. "You have a cavity." "I know, and I'd like you fill it."

—CAROLINE RHEA

Diapers

I hate changing my baby's diapers after he poops. I know exactly what he ate at day care. Yesterday, it was carrots. Tomorrow I'm hoping for long-stem roses.

—SHIRLEY LIPNER

Dieting

Never let your caloric intake exceed your white blood cell count.

—BETH DONAHUE

I went on that new fourteen-day diet, and all I lost was two weeks.

—SHEILA KAY

You know it's time to go on a diet when you're standing next to your car and get a ticket for double parking.

—TOTIE FIELDS

I hate dieting, but I've gotta do it. Last week I read about a diet that says, "Just eat half of everything you like," and I'm doing it diligently. Today I've eaten half a stick of celery, and half a pig.

—SALLY JACKSON

I've been on every diet in the world. I've been on Slim-Fast, yeah. For breakfast you have a shake. For lunch, you have a shake. For dinner, you kill anyone with food on their plate.

—ROSIE O'DONNELL

I had friends in high school who took diet pills. They talked me into trying it one time. They're like, "You won't want to eat anything." It didn't have that effect on me at all; I just ate really fast.

—SABRINA MATTHEWS

I think everyone should go on my Fuck It Diet. Basically, if I want something that has a lot of fat or carbs, I take a moment to go within, say "Fuck it," and eat. This works really well with my Fuck That Shit exercise program.

—MARGARET CHO

Differently Abled

You know the hardest thing about having cerebral palsy and being a woman? It's plucking your eyebrows. That's how I originally got pierced ears.

—GERI JEWELL

I was in a school for the retarded for two years before they found out I was hearing impaired. And they called *me* slow!

—KATHY BUCKLEY

Disclosure

Everybody feels they have to admit everything. Life has become a gigantic AA meeting. I was standing in the deli when this woman ordered coffee. The waiter asked, "Decaf?" and she took that as the chance to spill, "Oh yeah, I can't have caffeine, it has a very bad effect on my bowels, and I haven't been touched by another human being since 1981." And I'm thinking, "Oh, man, now I've got to top that."

—LAURA KIGHTLINGER

Divorce

I never even believed in divorce until after I got married.

—DIANE FORD

My marriage vows should have included the phrase, "Till debt do us part."

—KELLY SMITH

I got divorced recently. It was a mixed marriage. I'm human; he was Klingon.

—CAROL LEIFER

I'm divorced. I miss my husband, but I'm getting to be a better shot.

—SHEILA KAY

I'm not upset about my divorce. I'm only upset I'm not a widow.

—ROSEANNE BARR

I'm twenty-three and divorced. Maybe I should stop making important decisions with a Magic 8 Ball.

—CHRISTINA IRENE

My husband and I had a very messy divorce because there was a baby involved. Him. And I didn't want custody.

—WENDY LIEBMAN

When it comes to divorce, absence may not make the heart grow fonder, but it sure cuts down on the gunplay.

—EILEEN COURTNEY

I'm a divorced, single mother. That's like God saying to you, "Thank you for playing the Marriage Game. Sorry, you didn't win, but we have this lovely parting gift for you."

—CORY KAHANEY

I try too hard to be politically correct. Whenever I fill out an application for a credit card, under marital status, I write "pre-owned."

—FRAN CHERNOWSKY

It's hard to talk to divorced men, always sensitive from the divorce. They take things the wrong way. "Nice day, don't you think?" "I don't want to make a commitment." "Want half of my ice cream?" "I don't want half of anything anymore."

—ELAYNE BOOSLER

Doctors

I've got a doctor's appointment on Monday. I'm not sick or anything. It's just that I lost some weight, and I want someone to see me naked.

—TRACY SMITH

I went to the doctor and got my checkup. I hate getting undressed in front of him, but he is a good eye doctor.

—JENNY JONES

The doctor enters the examination room and says, "Okay, lay down."
I say, "Buy me a drink first, pig."

—JUDY TENUTA

I understand that the doctor had to spank me when I was born, but I really don't see any reason he had to call me a whore.

—SARAH SILVERMAN

I was having heart palpitations, so I went to a cardiologist. The nurse said the first visit would cost $350, but that would include a urine test, blood test, EKG, and rectal exam. A rectal exam. I said, "Hell, if this guy can see what's wrong with my heart through my ass, I'll give him four hundred."

—EILEEN KELLY

My father is a doctor, with the worst handwriting. He wrote me a note once excusing me from gym class. I gave it to my teacher, and she gave me all of her money.

—RITA RUDNER

Dogs

My husband and I are either going to buy a dog or have a child. We can't decide whether to ruin our carpet or ruin our lives.

—RITA RUDNER

I just got a new dog, Sammy. He's my fourth beagle. I get about fourteen or fifteen years out of a beagle. I've been married three times and I never get more than ten years out of a husband. I get a lot more mileage out of a beagle than a husband, and if the dogs want to go out and run around, I can have 'em neutered.

—MEG MALY

I've got a Chihuahua. They're good. If you lose one, just empty out your purse.

—JEAN CARROLL

I saw a dog food commercial advertising "30 percent less fat." I thought my dog spun in circles trying to catch her tail. I didn't know she was checking to see if her butt looks big.

—C. LYNN MITCHELL

I like driving around with my two dogs, especially on the freeways. I make them wear little hats so I can use the carpool lanes.

—MONICA PIPER

Some scientist spent twenty years in the lab inventing ice cream for dogs. He made it taste like vanilla, so it's hardly selling at all. If he'd made it taste like doody, dogs would be robbing stores with guns.

—ELAYNE BOOSLER

Oh, that dog! All he does is piddle. He's nothing but a fur-covered kidney that barks.

—PHYLLIS DILLER

I just got another puppy. I now have two. I didn't want another one, but I got her when my nieces were visiting. I thought we'd kill a couple hours at the pet store. There was a little girl puppy that looks like my puppy and the kids were playing with her. It's time to go, and I'm zipping up the three-year-old's coat and she's crying. I asked, "What's the matter, Julianna?" "Inside my heart I'm very much hurting, because we're leaving her in the cage and it looks like a jail and she didn't do anything wrong, and I'm so sorry we're not going to keep her, because I love you more than I love Mommy and Daddy." *Wrap it up.*

—ROSIE O'DONNELL

It's always the little dogs you see wearing sweaters. My neighbor's dog has a sweater, but he wears it just wrapped around his shoulders.

—ELLEN DEGENERES

Dolls

Barbie recently celebrated her fortieth anniversary. If only real women were shown the same respect. Barbie turns forty and she's a collector's item. A real woman turns forty and she's replaced by Skipper.

—JENNIFER VALLY

I never had a Barbie doll when I was growing up. I had a Tammy doll. She was like a brand-X Barbie, the doll that came with her own low self-esteem.

—CATHY LADMAN

A toy company is releasing Teacher Barbie. Apparently, it's like Malibu Barbie, only she can't afford the Corvette.

—STEPHANIE MILLER

Barbie and Ken are still a couple. This proves one thing: You don't need a penis to get a girl, just a really nice convertible.

—JENNIFER VALLY

There's this huge variety of Barbie dolls. They have Fun Time Barbie, Aviation Barbie. Oh, get this one: Gift-Giving Ken. You know, I really don't think this is going to prepare my niece for adult relationships. How about Date-Breaking Ken, I-Still-Live-with-My-Mother Ken, and Oh-You-Don't-Mind-if-My-Friend-Bob-Joins-Us Ken?

—CATHY LADMAN

Double Standard

There's a double standard, even today. A man can sleep around and sleep around, and nobody asks any questions. A woman, you make nineteen or twenty mistakes, right away you're a tramp.

—JOAN RIVERS

Dreams

Ever spend the night with someone and have a really bad dream about them? You wake up all furious and they have no idea why. "Why didn't you save me from Godzilla? He chased me all over that mall!"

—MONICA PIPER

Dressing

It takes women an hour to get dressed to go out; it takes guys five minutes. Ten minutes if they have to do the sniff test over the dirty pile of underwear in the corner.

—MARYELLEN HOOPER

Men don't feel the urge to get married as quickly as women do because their clothes all button and zip in the front. Women's dresses usually button and zip in the back. We need men emotionally and sexually, but we also need men to help us get dressed.

—RITA RUDNER

You won't get a man to do what you want by dressing sexy. If you want a man to listen to you, dress like his mother.

—DIANA JORDAN

Dressing Rooms

We go into these little cells, with mirrors every place, and very cruel lighting. So we can see exactly what's wrong with our body, from every conceivable angle. I think after you leave those rooms they should offer you some type of counseling. Or at least have a sticker on the mirror that says, CAUTION: OBJECTS IN MIRROR MAY APPEAR LARGER.

—RITA RUDNER

Drinking

I've been drinking a lot, and a friend suggested that I go to an AA meeting. When I got there they had a pamphlet near the door that listed the ten signs that you may have a drinking problem. One of the items on the pamphlet said, "Does drinking affect your family?" I'm thinking "Hell, drinking *started* my family."

—JENNIFER VALLY

When you're out drinking you want to be responsible, but you always have that one drunk friend who says, "Have another drink. I'll follow you home." I never understood the logic behind that. We're going to have this drunk caravan flying down the highway. The only thing it's good for is that your drunken friend will be able to tell the cops what happened, "I was following her, until she hit that tree."

—WANDA SYKES

My parents think DWI laws are for wimps. They're really annoyed that they can have their driver's license taken away for driving a car while drunk. But they found a way around it. "Warm up the tractor, we're going to the bar."

—KELLI DUNHAM

I like my men like I like my Pop-Tarts: toasted.

—CHRISTINA IRENE

I like to get drunk. All the way to throwing-up time. Then I don't like that no more. That's when I start saying real stupid things like, "I shouldn't have had that last one." Like that's the one that did it. The first seventeen I had don't count? That last one fucked me up.

—MARSHA WARFIELD

When I was in college we used to watch *The Love Boat*. We played a drinking game where everyone picks a character at the beginning of the show and whenever that person appeared in the show you would take a drink. You could always tell who the alcoholics in your group were because they would say, "I want to be the boat."

—MARGARET CHO

Some people say that a drunk woman is worse than a drunk man. I don't believe that. I don't care who you are, if you throw up on my shoes, I'm gonna punch your lights out.

—MARSHA WARFIELD

I have cerebral palsy, and I don't understand why people will go out of their way to drink so they walk like me.

—GERI JEWELL

Young guys love to get wasted. Don't! It makes you impotent. Being with a young hottie who can't get it up is like ordering a banana split with all nuts and no banana.

—ELAINE PELINO

After a night out: What did I say? Who did I make out with? Why do these muscles hurt?

—JANEANE GAROFALO

I can't think of anything worse after a night of drinking than waking up next to someone and not being able to remember their name, or how you met, or why they're dead.

—LAURA KIGHTLINGER

Driving

Always wear your seat belt while driving, or else you'll have to paint pictures with your teeth.

—JUDY TENUTA

I am the worst driver. Let's just say I always wear clean underwear. I should drive a hearse and cut out the middle man.

—WENDY LIEBMAN

One of the things I love about driving is when truckers beep at me. But I don't know if it's because they think I'm cute, or if it's because I taped a sign in my window that says, "Honk if you like chili-cheese dogs."

—CHRISTINA IRENE

When guys hit on me, sometimes it can be annoying. Like when I'm driving there's always that annoying guy telling me to pull over, and if I don't he gets all desperate and puts on his siren. And he always asks, "Do you know why I pulled you over?" Yeah, because I'm a girl.

—CHANTEL RAE

I've become so vain. I went through one of those traffic lights that takes a picture when you go through a red light. I hated the picture, so I went through the light again. By the third time, I was pretty confident in front of the camera.

—LEMAIRE

Sometimes when I'm driving I get so angry at inconsiderate drivers that I want to scream at them. But then I remember how insignificant that is, and I thank God that I have a car, and my health, and gas. That was phrased wrong, normally you wouldn't say, "Thank God I have gas."

—ELLEN DEGENERES

Driving on the freeway is like hand washing my delicate clothes. It's a big hassle, it takes longer than I expect, and I end up with my panties in a wad.

—LESLEY WAKE

I had this dream that I was, like, driving down the freeway and slamming into everyone, just slamming into them. From side to side to side, right to left, all the way down the freeway. Not hurting anyone, though, just knocking the phones out of their hands.

—LAURA KIGHTLINGER

I hate driving, and I hate when people honk at me. Unless I'm making a left turn. Then I like it because that's how I know it's time to turn.

—RITA RUDNER

I don't actually want to raise a child, I just want to be able to use the car pool lane. But I could fake it. Put a baby seat back there, throw a doll in it. Who's going to know? But what if I got pulled over, what would I do? Start crying, and tell them the real one died.

—MARGARET SMITH

My big fear: driving behind a truck with those big iron rebars. Truck stops, the bar goes right through my forehead. It doesn't kill me, they can't remove it, and I have to accessorize it.

—CARRIE SNOW

When my husband and I are in the car, I usually let him drive. Because when I drive, he has a tendency to bite the dashboard.

—RITA RUDNER

Signs on the freeway are funny. ORANGE CONES MEAN MEN AT WORK. What else could orange cones mean? Psychedelic witches embedded in asphalt?

—KAREN BABBITT

Drugs

My cousin Jacoy is a crack addict and he's always trying to borrow money. But I don't play that because lending a crack head twenty bucks is like loaning out one of your good knives to O. J. Simpson— you're never going to see it again.

—RENÉ HICKS

California is drugs, drugs, drugs. If it's white and it's on the table they're going to sniff it. I have a friend who OD-ed at the beauty parlor from sniffing dandruff.

—JOAN RIVERS

I don't do drugs, because I saw what it did to my friends. I'd get stoned, and they'd look really weird to me.

—WENDY LIEBMAN

My teenage daughter comes home every night with her friends, they go in her room, close the door, and then they light incense. Like I don't know what's going on in there. Like I think there's a Zen Buddhist meeting in my apartment.

—CORY KAHANEY

People say, "You need to do ecstasy. Ecstasy is great." I know for a fact that if I were to do ecstasy, I would end up alone in a corner humping a houseplant for five hours.

—BECKY DONOHUE

I think it's super sad when people are too old and addicted to pot. I was at a party and this guy with a gray, greasy ponytail and a bald spot comes up to me and says, "Hey, man, I got a new roach clip!" It's so pathetic, I want to say, "Grow up! Be an alcoholic!"

—CATHRYN MICHON

The best mind-altering drug is truth.

—LILY TOMLIN

Dry Cleaners

I put my clothes in the cleaners and then don't have the money to get them out. It's like they're in jail waiting on me to spring 'em.

—PAULA POUNDSTONE

A good place to meet a man is at the dry cleaner. These men usually have jobs and bathe.

—RITA RUDNER

Eating

I have a friend who's a macrobiotic. She doesn't eat meat, chicken, fish, white flour, sugar, or preservatives. She's pale, sickly, and exhausted just from looking for something to eat. She can eat wicker.

—PAULA POUNDSTONE

I come from this big meat-eating family. We do shots of gravy with dinner.

—SUZANNE WESTENHOEFER

Skinny people piss me off. Especially when they say things like, "You know, sometimes I forget to eat." Now I've forgotten my address, my mother's maiden name, my money, and my keys. But I've never forgotten to eat. You have to be a special kind of stupid to forget to eat. In that case, you don't *deserve* to eat.

—MARSHA WARFIELD

Did you ever just sit around and eat and drink for about three years? I had a good reason. I was waiting for Publishers Clearing House.

—MARILYN

Eating Disorders

Anorexia is just another word for nothing left to lose.

—JOY BEHAR

I went to a conference for bulimics and anorexics. It was a nightmare: The bulimics ate the anorexics. But it was okay, because they were back again in ten minutes.

—MONICA PIPER

I'd hate to be a member of Overeaters Anonymous. It's not like Alcoholics Anonymous, where you can hear some wild testimony of drunken debauchery. How exciting can OA testimony be? It's not like you are ever going to hear, "Wow, I'm sorry. I was so full last night I don't remember meeting you."

—LAURA KIGHTLINGER

I've decided that perhaps I'm bulimic and just keep forgetting to purge.

—PAULA POUNDSTONE

Elevators

Ever do this? You walk up to an elevator, somebody is there, they've already pushed the button. But you think, "He couldn't have pushed it correctly, I'll push it myself. *Now* the elevator will come."

—ELLEN DEGENERES

I was in Dayton, Ohio, and walked by the Otis Elevator Building. It's one floor. Apparently they know something we don't.

—PAULA POUNDSTONE

Emotions

Always keep your anger bottled up. You might need a bottle of anger someday when friends come by and don't leave.

—LAURA KIGHTLINGER

I've been on an emotional roller coaster lately. The other day my mood ring exploded.

—JANINE DITULLIO

Employment

I was a ballerina. I had to quit after I injured a groin muscle. It wasn't mine.

—RITA RUDNER

The government is spending a lot of money studying the nursing shortage. I'm a nurse, and I think I can save them a few bucks on researching this great mystery. It's simple: Nurses have bachelor's degrees, and we clean up doody.

—KELLI DUNHAM

I used to work at the International House of Pancakes. I know what you are thinking. "Why? How's that possible?" But you set your goals and go for them. I made it happen. It was the worst job I ever had in my entire life. When people were rude to me, I touched their eggs. It's true. I flipped them over in the back with my hand. Four times. They didn't know, but I felt better.

—PAULA POUNDSTONE

Engagement

I was engaged once when I was twenty-three, but I had to call it off. It turned out I wasn't pregnant after all.

—FRANCES DILORINZO

Being engaged sucks. I was engaged for a year. If dating is like shopping, being engaged is like having a guy put you on layaway. Like saying, "I know I want it. I just want to delay taking it home as long as possible."

—KRIS MCGAHA

When my fiancé proposed it was very romantic. He turned off the TV. Well, he muted it. During the commercial.

—WENDY LIEBMAN

I had a nasty engagement that gave me pre-divorce jitters.

—BONNIE CHEESEMAN

Before we got engaged he never farted. Now it's a second language.

—CAROLINE RHEA

You ever notice the word *engaged* has the word *gag* in the middle of it? Just something to think about, ladies.

—ROSIE O'DONNELL

Environmentalism

I have tended to view my acts of conservation as some sort of retirement-account deposit. As if, when the earth appears drained of every last bit of fossil fuel, there will be a few more full gas tanks set aside for me because of the time I walked to my therapist instead of driving.

—PAULA POUNDSTONE

I just got junk mail from this organization that wants me to save the forest. I sent them back a letter saying, "Stop sending me the junk mail and save the forest yourself."

—LINDA HERSKOVIC

Remember when you were considered an environmentalist when you didn't throw junk out of the car window? I sure do miss that happier, simpler time.

—PAULA POUNDSTONE

I'm doing what I can to help the environment. I started a compost pile. It's in the backseat of my car.

—JANINE DITULLIO

Ethnicity

People always want to judge you based on your ethnic background. It's stupid. For instance, if a white guy likes rap, he's trying to be black. If a black guy gets a job, he's trying to be white.

—AISHA TYLER

The only sort of Asian role model I had in American culture when I was growing up was Hello Kitty. I don't want to model myself on Hello Kitty: She doesn't have a mouth. She can't even say anything back when you say, "Hello, Kitty!"

—MARGARET CHO

I'm biracial or, for those of you that fill out those loan applications, I'm "Other." I'm half black, half Puerto Rican. In Los Angeles, that makes me Mexican. In Miami, it makes me Cuban, and in Mississippi it makes me dead.

—LYDIA NICOLE

I'm not politically correct; I still say "black." Because "African-American" doesn't give you no bonus. It doesn't make your life any easier. You don't see black people standing around saying, "Ohhh, yeah, African-American, mmm-hmm-hmm; man, I tell you, this beats the hell out of being black. We should have made the switch years ago."

—WANDA SYKES

The only way that I know that I'm Cuban is I have a really bad temper, and I can make a boat out of a plastic bag.

—SHARON HOUSTON

Jewish people can look at other Jewish people and tell that they're Jewish. It's a phenomenon. It's just like black people can pick other black people out of a crowd.

—JUDY GOLD

I'm Irish and Dutch. Which means my idea of a good time is to get drunk and drive my car into a windmill.

—KRIS MCGAHA

I come from a large Jewish family: two children.

—KAREN HABER

My father is a German Jew, and my mother is a French Jew. So that makes me just really lucky to be here.

—JACKIE WOLLNER

Men look at me and think I'm going to walk on their backs or something. I tell them, "The only time I'll walk on your back is if there's something on the other side of you I want."

—MARGARET CHO

People don't know a lot about Puerto Ricans. When you're born in Puerto Rico you're automatically an American citizen. Some people get pissed off. They ask me, "Let me get this straight: You don't have to swim rivers, cross deserts, and climb mountains to get here?" And I say, "Well, yes. But when a Puerto Rican does that we call it camping."

—CATHERINE FRANCO

I'm a WASP, a White Anglo-Saxon Protestant, and actually, a lot of my people are doing really well.

—PENELOPE LOMBARD

Euthanasia

If I'm ever stuck on a respirator or a life support system I definitely want to be unplugged. But not until I'm down to a size eight.

—HENRIETTE MANTEL

Evolution

I don't understand evolution. If we came from monkeys, why are there still monkeys? What, they couldn't make it over the hump? George W. Bush made it, what's up with their raggedy asses?

—KATHLEEN MADIGAN

Exercise

Whenever I read anything, it says, "Consult your doctor before doing any exercise." Does anybody do that? I kind of think my doctor has people coming in with serious problems. I don't think I should call him and say, "Hi, this is Rita. I'm thinking of bending at the waist."

—RITA RUDNER

Aerobics went from high impact to low impact. I hope they next find a way for us to do it sitting down eating and drinking a beer. But then they'll have to call it bowling.

—DIANE FORD

I'm so tired of exercising. I think five thousand sit-ups should be pretty much permanent. You should be at home, you're on your last and final jumping jack, and you get that phone call, "Congratulations! You have completed the exercise portion of your life. Welcome to the incessant eating section."

—JANN KARAM

I really should work out; my ass is pushing down my socks.

—LEMAIRE

If you "power walk," can you "power sit"?

—ELLEN DEGENERES

I don't like to exercise unless it's in one of those classes. I'm Jewish and we like to suffer in a group.

—DAVA KRAUSE

My trainer says that it's best to have a female trainer because male trainers often say inappropriate things to their clients. I'm thinking, where can I sign up for those guys?

—BONNIE CHEESEMAN

My grandmother began walking five miles a day when she was eighty-two. Now we don't know where the hell she is.

—ELLEN DEGENERES

I'm a personal trainer for senior citizens. I think it's so important that I work with the elderly. Mostly because I'm not that physically fit.

—PENELOPE LOMBARD

I don't think jogging is healthy, especially morning jogging. If morning joggers knew how tempting they looked to morning motorists, they would stay home and do sit-ups.

—RITA RUDNER

At this point, at my age, it's just maintenance. I'm just trying to stop my ass from going to Brazil without me.

—SUE MURPHY

You know, I really don't think I need buns of steel. I'd be happy with buns of cinnamon.

—ELLEN DEGENERES

Married people don't have to exercise because our attitude is, "They've seen us naked already, and they like it."

—CAROL MONTGOMERY

I bought Rollerblades. I go out one day, and Rollerblade for five hours because I was going to skate away a decade of beer and pizza in a single afternoon.

—SABRINA MATTHEWS

I'm not working out. My philosophy: no pain, no pain.

—CAROL LEIFER

I go running when I have to. When the ice cream truck is doing sixty.

—WENDY LIEBMAN

I thought Spinning was this exotic new exercise at the gym, but it's just a bunch of people riding stationary bicycles. Yeah, and they're renaming the StairMaster, "Stomping."

—DENISE MUNRO ROBB

I took an aggression training course. The Basic Bitch Workout. Now I'm certified. I give new meaning to that time of the month. I no longer just get cramps; now I can give them.

—S. RACHEL LOVEY

I know I should work out, but I don't so much. I don't mind sweating, though. As long as I don't have to move. Like in a sauna. Or a good audit.

—WENDY LIEBMAN

My boyfriend is a fitness trainer, very enthusiastic. He loves doing bench presses and squats. I have my favorite exercises, too: The Refrigerator Lunge, followed by the Microwave Push.

—ANDI RHOADS

Ex-husbands

Never bad-mouth your ex-husband to your kids. Because if you do, then you ruin the moment when they figure it out all by themselves.

—CORY KAHANEY

My ex-husband is suing me for custody of the kids, so now I have to go to court and fight him because my lawyer says it would look really bad if I don't.

—ROSEANNE BARR

My ex-husband was a drummer, and he had this nervous habit of hitting on things, like my girlfriends. Yeah, he was always banging on something.

—LEMAIRE

Even though my ex-husband wouldn't talk to me at my daughter's wedding, he still expected me to run his errands. He gave our son his tuxedo for me to take back. I returned it to the swimming pool.

—DARYL HOGUE

Regarding her ex-husband: In lovemaking, what he lacked in size, he made up for in speed.

—ROSEANNE BARR

I miss my ex-husband. We still talk, we reminisce about the good old day.

—WENDY LIEBMAN

Faking It

Guys wonder why we fake it. It's called "time management." I don't need to be up all night working on something that's not going to happen; you're just cutting into my sleep time. He's working hard at making something happen, you already know it ain't gonna happen, and you glance at the clock, "Shoot, it's 1:30 in the morning and I got to get up at six. To hell with this—*Oh yes! Oh yes, baby!*"

—WANDA SYKES

Fallopian Tubes

I would like to wear my fallopian tubes on the outside because they're so pretty.

—CATHY LADMAN

Family

I've thought about having a family. I just haven't seen any that really appeal to me.

—LAURA KIGHTLINGER

Blood may be thicker than water, but it is still sticky, unpleasant, and generally nauseating.

—JANEANE GAROFALO

I love my family, but I hate family reunions. Family reunions are that time when you come face to face with your family tree and realize some branches need to be cut.

—RENÉ HICKS

Nobody in my family is related. My sister and I are both adopted. And my parents, thank God, aren't related, either.

—KATHLEEN KANZ

I walked into a family reunion and thought, "Ugh, I'm getting my tubes tied."

—CATHY LADMAN

My parents did a really scary thing recently. They bought a Winnebago. This means they can pull up in front of my house anytime now and just live there.

—PAULA POUNDSTONE

My family is so dysfunctional that I looked up the word *dysfunctional* in the dictionary. There was a picture of my mother.

—PAULARA R. HAWKINS

When I was four, my mom forgot me on the sidewalk once, by accident. At least I like to believe it was an accident, because when the police officer brought me back home, my family had moved.

—CECILE LUBRANI

I love my husband, I love my children, but I want something more. Like a life.

—ROSEANNE BARR

My family is really boring. They have a coffee table book called "Pictures We Took Just to Use Up the Rest of the Film."

—PENELOPE LOMBARD

I'm a godmother. That's a great thing, to be a godmother. She calls me God for short; that's cute. I taught her that.

—ELLEN DEGENERES

My mother is Mormon and my father is Moslem. I've got polygamy on both sides. My mother's great-great-grandfather had three wives, my father's great-grandfather had four. My family tree is like a diagram of the heart. All lines come from one organ.

—NATASHA AHANIN

I come from a typical American family. Me, my mother, her third husband, his daughter from a second marriage, my stepsister, her illegitimate son.

—CAROL HENRY

Family Values

I'm so sick of hearing about family values. Most of us are in therapy because of our families. I'm surprised you don't hear about more calls to 911: "Help me, I'm in a family. Get me out of here!"

—JUDY CARTER

If I hear the words "family values" one more time, I'm going to have to go home and kill my parents.

—LAURA KIGHTLINGER

Fantasies

I'm a modern woman; most of my fantasies are of more sleep.

—LAURA HAYDEN

What's the number-one fantasy for most guys? Two women. Fellows, I think that's a bit lofty. Come on, if you can't satisfy that one woman, why you want to piss off another one? Why have two angry women in bed with you at the same time?

—WANDA SYKES

Fashion

There are weird rules for girls; we get all the uncomfortable crap. We get all the S&M clothes, like the high heels that make us easier to hunt.

—SUE MURPHY

Never let a panty line show around your ankle.

—JOAN RIVERS

You never hear a man say, "I'm so embarrassed. There's another man here wearing a black tuxedo." They're happy if they all look alike. It means they haven't made a mistake.

—RITA RUDNER

Fathers

I was raised by my father since birth. He's been both mother and father to me: I call him Smother. He still lactates whenever he hears a baby cry.

—KAITLIN COLOMBO

My dad liked to take everything apart and put it back together, which made my life hell. How would you like to go around explaining why your Barbie has a lazy eye?

—LIVIA SQUIRES

My father was a gambler and an alcoholic. He was also very vain. So one day he gave up his vices to save up enough money for a hair transplant. Two days after the transplant was complete, he got drunk and on a twenty-dollar bet he shaved his head. So I owe him twenty dollars.

—MARGARET SMITH

When I was a baby, my father used to throw me up in the air and then answer the phone.

—RITA RUDNER

My dad used to say to me when I was a kid, "Eat your peas. It'll put hair on your chest." Okay, I'm five, I'm Italian. I already have hair on my chest.

—MARIA MENOZZI

My father was a cop, so dating was a nightmare. I could handle the police escort, but the bullhorn from the helicopter was a bit much: "Son, keep your hands on the steering wheel where we can see them."

—SANDI SELVI

My dad's so cheap. He's always yelling at me, "Look at you, spending money, you're such a big shot." Oh yeah, buying food, paying rent. I'm just showing off.

—CATHY LADMAN

I'm a grown woman, but my father still thinks I know nothing about my car. He always asks me, "You changing the oil every 3,000?" "Yes, Dad. I'm also putting sugar in the gas tank. That way my exhaust smells like cotton candy."

—MIMI GONZALEZ

My father is so impatient. He stands in front of the microwave going, "*C'mon!* It's been ten seconds! I don't have all minute!"

—CATHY LADMAN

When I think of my dad, I get this sort of Obi-Wan Kenobi voice in my head, but instead of giving me words of wisdom and advice, it just says things like, "Ow, my back! Where's my Vicodin?" Or, "Pull my finger. Just pull it."

—LORI CHAPMAN

If you ever want to torture my dad, tie him up and right in front of him, refold a road map incorrectly.

—CATHY LADMAN

Father's Day: I hate this occasion. I can never find the right card, because they are all too nice.

—MARGARET SMITH

Fatigue

I don't know if I'm just tired or lazy. Today I fell asleep during a massage. That I was giving.

—SIMONE ALEXANDER

Feet

I have big feet, which means I have a big uterus.

—ALEX HOUSE

Female Impersonators

Gay men in drag think it's glamorous being a woman, that it's all about the dress and makeup. Hey, buddy, if you really want to impersonate a woman shove a tampon up your wazoo every month, give birth, and take a cut in pay.

—MICHELE BALAN

Feminine Hygiene Products

We need to do an immediate hostile takeover of a sanitary-pad company. These things are getting so expensive you'd think they taste good.

—KATE CLINTON

My mom died when I was ten years old. When I was thirteen I got my period, and I had to discuss it with my dad. Hard for any kid. "Dad, I have to go to the store to *get some tampons*." "Harpoons? What the hell does a girl your age need with harpoons?"

—ROSIE O'DONNELL

Feminity

People say to me, "You're not very feminine." Well, they can just suck my dick.

—ROSEANNE BARR

Feminism

When I say I'm a feminist, I make it clear I'm not anti-male, just anti-asshole. Having been an asshole myself, I realize that it's a gender-free concept.

—MIMI GONZALEZ

I don't agree with feminists. I saw a feminist on TV saying "If women ruled the world, there'd be no crime, no pollution, and no war." I'm thinking, "Great. What happens if there's a spider?"

—LIVIA SQUIRES

Rush Limbaugh calls feminists "feminazis." But having Rush Limbaugh call you a Nazi is like having Kato Kaelin call you a freeloader.

—JACKIE WOLLNER

Feminists miss the big picture. They want us to be concerned about the fact that Barbie, if she were a real woman, would have no internal organs because her waist is too small. I say Barbie's got nothing to complain about in the missing-organ department compared to Ken.

—CATHRYN MICHON

I wanted to be a feminist in high school, but my boyfriend wouldn't let me.

—DENISE MUNRO ROBB

I don't call myself a feminist. I call myself a killer bitch.

—ROSEANNE BARR

Fired

I've been fired a few times in my life. And that's fine. In a lot of cases, it's only a little worse than getting hired.

—LAURA KIGHTLINGER

I got fired from being a receptionist for putting people on hold for no reason. "Please hold." "Can you hold some more?" "What are you holding now?"

—DIANE FORD

I was a New York state employee and after nine years of dedicated service they fired me for no reason. One day they just marched into my office, woke me up, and told me to go home.

—NIKKI CARR

Fish

I have fish for pets. That's what I have. Goldfish. It was originally for the stress thing. They say if you watch fish, it helps you relax, to fall asleep. Which explains why I always doze off when I'm snorkeling.

—ELLEN DEGENERES

My parents never wanted me to be upset about anything. They couldn't tell me when a pet had died. Once I woke up and my goldfish was gone. I asked, "Mom? Where's Fluffy?" She said, "He ran away."

—RITA RUDNER

Fishing

My husband is totally into fishing. He enters tournaments and they cost $600. Well, actually, it's $100 for the tournament and $500 for beer.

—FRANCES DILORINZO

My ex-husband is the kind of guy who would watch a fishing show on television and pay attention to it.

—BRETT BUTLER

Flirting

My biggest problem with dating is that I have no game. Some women can just bat their eyes and men come running. The men just keep popping up one after another. It's like they have a magical man-filled Pez dispenser.

—LORI GIARNELLA

Flying

I know that experts say you're more likely to get hurt crossing the street than you are flying, but that doesn't make me feel any less frightened of flying. If anything, it makes me more afraid of crossing the street.

—ELLEN DEGENERES

I called to change my airline ticket. I'd paid $620 to go to New York, so you'd think I could get a little assistance. But apparently I'd purchased the immutable, fascist you-can-just-sit-in-your-seat-and-shut-your-hole ticket. They say, "How can I help you?" But they don't. Why don't they just say what they really mean? "Hi, this Donna. Give it a rest."

—JANEANE GAROFALO

There's nothing random about the random search at the airport. You go to the gate and they're standing there with a Sherwin-Williams paint chart. If your ass is darker than khaki, you getting searched.

—WANDA SYKES

Security is ridiculous: "Take off your hat, take off your coat, take off your belt, take off your shoes." I said, "If you make me take off one more piece of clothing, there had better be guys over there with twenty-dollar bills to stuff in my panties."

—RENÉ HICKS

On planes salads are two pieces of dead lettuce and salad dressing that comes in that astronaut package. As soon as you open it, it's on your neighbor's lap. "Could I just dip my lettuce, ma'am? Hmm, that's a lovely skirt. What is that, silk?"

—ELLEN DEGENERES

I was flying and this guy was sitting next to me, and I could tell he really wanted me—to shut up. Because he kept saying, "*Shut up!*" I'm chatting and chatting and he's busy, flying the plane. And he's, like, very focused, on that bottle of vodka.

—WENDY LIEBMAN

I'd better not get too comfortable in my three-quarter-of-an-inch recline because toward the end of the flight, the flight attendant is going to say, "You're going to have to put your seat in the upright position for landing." They're so adamant about that every single time, like that's gonna make a difference. Because if we crash, the investigators are going to say, "Oh, that's a shame, her seat was reclined. When will they learn? What was that, thirty thousand feet? She could have made that. Sheesh. If only she'd been upright."

—ELLEN DEGENERES

I'm afraid of planes; I don't trust the oxygen mask. The little orange cup—attached to that bag that's full of nothing. Maybe I'm cynical. I don't even think that it's an oxygen mask. I think it's more to just muffle the screams.

—RITA RUDNER

I'm terrified of dying in a plane crash. I'd hate the thought that peanuts would be my last meal.

—TANYA LUCKERATH

I was at the airport in the baggage claim area waiting for my bag. There was all these suitcases going by, and one lone red bra drifting down the conveyer belt. Everyone was laughing and I was like, "That's mine." Unfortunately, I wasn't the only one who thought that. There was pulling and tugging and screaming, but eventually he backed off.

—WENDY SPERO

Food

They have flavored bagels now. This is just wrong. Pesto bagels, raisin-walnut-strawberry-streusel bagels. That's not a bagel. That's a doughnut having a bad day.

—JANET ROSEN

Why is it whenever I get a fortune cookie, it always says stuff like, "You wouldn't know happiness if it crawled up your ass"?

—SHARI BECKER

I love Chinese food. I have my own chopsticks. They have my initials on the top and Velcro on the bottom.

—RITA RUDNER

I use ice cream as a natural antidepressant. I call it dairy-Prozac.

—MEG MALY

Ever notice that soup for one is eight aisles away from party mix?

—ELAYNE BOOSLER

I was looking at a box of mac and cheese and I noticed that at the bottom of the ingredients list, they listed "possible ingredients." I freaked out and checked the cans and boxes of food in my kitchen, and they all had "possible ingredients." Possibly contains traces of peanuts, Yellow Food Dye #8, the list went on and on. But anything is possible. Maybe they're just taunting us. "This peanut butter may contain toxic chemicals and dirty gym socks. We're not sure, and frankly we're too lazy to look for it."

—ROSIE TRAN

I've been to six stores trying to buy a can of rat hairs and animal impurities and every can had tuna fish in it.

—LILY TOMLIN

I look at rice cakes and think, "Who woke up one morning and said, 'Packing material, pressed into a disc, *yummy!*'"

—SABRINA MATTHEWS

Tofu! Why do people eat tofu? I throw out my old sponges.

—KAREN WILLIAMS

I don't understand these people who go to the co-op and buy all sorts of "healthy" junk food. Yesterday, at Whole Foods the woman in front of me bought organic cheese doodles. Does she think that organic cholesterol is good for you? Her organic cottage cheese ass doesn't look any better than the one I got at McDonald's.

—JENNIFER POST

I just gave up dairy, caffeine, and sugar because I was feeling sluggish, tired, and anxious. Now I have a lot more energy to feel angry and deprived.

—JENNIFER SIEGAL

You get those people who can't eat anything. No sugar. I don't know about you, but I'm not naturally that sweet; I need some sugar. No preservatives. That's when I really put my foot down. We live in the threat of a nuclear holocaust; I want as many preservatives holding my thin ass together as possible.

—KAREN RIPLEY

If a man prepares dinner for you and the salad contains three or more types of lettuce, he is serious.

—RITA RUDNER

Why is there an expiration date on yogurt? It's bad milk with fruit in it. It should say "Worse, after August 3rd."

—EILEEN KELLY

Food Poisoning

I had food poisoning once. It was incredibly debilitating, and it really made me hate my idiot friends. I'm, like, dying on the bed, and the phone rings, "What's wrong, Judy?" "I have food poisoning." "What did you eat?" Which is the last thing I want to think about. "I had mahimahi, it was delicious. Actually it was better the second time, on the way up. I tasted stuff I had no idea was in the recipe."

—JUDY GOLD

Forgetfulness

Did you ever walk into a room and forget why you walked in? I think that's how dogs spend their lives.

—SUE MURPHY

Friends

When I was a girl I only had two friends, and they were imaginary. And they would only play with each other.

—RITA RUDNER

My friends are like family to me, because they're so needy and demented.

—JANET ROSEN

When you have a man in your life, you tend to neglect your women friends. They call you, and you're like, "I have a man. I'm sorry you're lonely. Get a dog, buy some batteries, and call me next week, okay? I'm busy."

—MONIQUE MARVEZ

Men, I'm telling you: If you have a woman and she has a best friend, they have drawn your penis on a napkin at Denny's.

—MONIQUE MARVEZ

She's my best friend. She thinks I'm too thin, and I think she's a natural blonde.

—CARRIE SNOW

I love my friends. Without them, I'd be the most screwed-up person I know.

—MARGOT BLACK

Friends are just enemies who don't have enough guts to kill you.

—JUDY TENUTA

You need to have a stupid girlfriend so that on a bad day you can call her. "Tanya, I'm having a bad day, tell me something stupid you've done. You caught on fire, and you tried to put it out with *alcohol*?!"

—ELLEN CLEGHORNE

I used to be the unpaid shrink to all my friends. They'd call and complain, and I'd say, "No, honey, you're not a loser, you're a runner-up."

—JANET ROSEN

Funeral Homes

The other day I drove by a funeral home with a clock on it. Is that pressure or what? Tick! Tick!

—ROXANE LARIMORE

Funerals

Why do dead people get to ride in such nice cars? That can piss you off if you're on the bus.

—MARSHA WARFIELD

I'm not afraid of death. It's the makeover at the undertaker's that scares me. They try to make you look as lifelike as possible, which defeats the whole purpose. It's hard to feel bad for somebody who looks better than you do.

—ANITA WISE

I know one woman who had her husband cremated and then mixed his ashes with grass and smoked him. She said, "That's the best he's made me feel for years."

—MAUREEN MURPHY

I got a coupon in the mail: ash burial at sea, $478. What an affordable way to die. The only thing is, I don't want my ashes scattered at sea. I want them thrown on all the people who have ever blown smoke in my face. Let's see if their dry cleaners can get that out.

—CATHY LADMAN

My husband lost his job at a cemetery because he used to practice ventriloquism at funerals.

—PHYLLIS DILLER

Fur

I bought a fur coat about ten years ago, and I feel so guilty I'm trying to revive it.

—RITA RUDNER

Furniture

I filled out a rental application that asked, "Do you own any liquid-filled furniture?" Couldn't they just have said water bed? How many other forms of liquid-filled furniture are there? "Yeah, I have a beer couch, will that be a problem?"

—LISA GOICH

G, H, I

Garage Sales

There's nothing more pathetic on earth than a garage sale. You sit in your driveway with all your crap, and it's not even your good crap.

—SUE MURPHY

Gardening

Gardening is so complex. I can only grow simple plants like mildew. My friend has a green thumb. She makes salad, it takes root. She has a hedge made out of broccoli.

—JEANNIE DIETZ

I've killed so many plants. I walked into a nursery once and my face was on a wanted poster.

—RITA RUDNER

thumb. I can't even get mold to grow on last

—JOHNNYE JONES GIBSON

Gas Stations

I hate self-service gas stations so much. I was all dressed up once going to a formal affair, so I was standing there in the middle of the night, in an evening gown, pumping gas. I looked like the gas fairy.

—RITA RUDNER

My gas station had a sign that read PLEASE PAY WITH YOUR SMALLEST BILL. So I gave them the white dollar bill from my Monopoly set. The cops caught up with me a couple blocks later, but I was in luck. I also had the "Get out of Jail Free" card.

—KATE ZANNONI

Gas Tanks

My car has this feature that I guess is standard, because it was on my last car, too. It has a rotating gas tank. Whatever side of the pump I pull up to, it's on the other side.

—RITA RUDNER

Gifts

Men are so cheap these days. Whatever happened to guys bringing women chocolates or flowers? I've reached the point where the grim reaper could show up at my door and I'd be like, "Oh my God, you brought me a scythe! That's so sweet."

—JENÉE

Not romantic, my husband. Do you know what he gave me for M
Day? A George Foreman grill. I gave it back to him for Fathers Day,
a sort of forceful upward motion.

—SANDI SELVI

I was dating this one guy and he was so nice, he was bringing me
flowers and cards and candy. And I think that's annoying. When they
bring flowers, I've got to find a vase now, great. All I have is an old Big
Gulp cup.

—MARGARET CHO

For my thirty-first birthday, my boyfriend bought me a treadmill. He's
dead now. So young, so tragic, so clueless.

—MEL FINE

Girl Scouts

I was expelled from the Girl Scouts for creativity. They had another
name for it: pyromania.

—AURORA COTSBECK

I learned an awful lot as a Brownie. I learned how to start a campfire
with two sticks—and a match. And how to survive in the woods on
only five dollars a day.

—DONNA JEAN YOUNG

was nothing. God said, "Let there be light!" And
'as still nothing, but you could see it a whole
.. better.

—ELLEN DEGENERES

Men made God in their image, and he's a deadbeat dad. Never sends
money, doesn't come to visit, can't get him on the phone. And poor
Earth, she's our single mother. Who can blame her for letting off steam
with tornados, hurricanes, and earthquakes?

—MIMI GONZALEZ

I asked God what was in store for me today, like I do every morning.
And he said, "Well, not so much that you couldn't turn your alarm off
another five times." And I said, "Thank you, Lord; that's what I was
thinking."

—LAURA KIGHTLINGER

I'm glad God gave the Ten Commandments to a man. A woman would
have thought, "I know that's what he said, but I don't think that's what
he meant."

—DIANE NICHOLS

Basically, my husband has two beliefs in life. He believes in God, and he
believes that when the gas gauge is on empty, he still has a quarter of
a tank. He thinks that "E" stands for "Eh, there's still some left."

—RITA RUDNER

Going With

Remember "going with" someone when you were a little girl? When I was in fifth grade, Bucky McGinn came up to me on the playground and asked me to go with him. I said yes. And that was it; I never ever heard from him again. As far as I'm concerned, we're still going. I don't care if he is married with two kids.

—MARY GALLAGHER

I think dating was a lot easier when we were younger. Remember going together? Where were we going? Between the ages of ten and twelve our options were pretty limited, but everyone was going with someone. Everyone but me. But back in the day, boys called me . . . about homework. After the third or fourth call a night, the realization hit. Ohmigod, I'm the smart girl! Might as well stick a hump on my back and throw me in a bell tower. No one wants to go with the smart girl. I could have been born beautiful, but *nooo*, I had to be born smart. Like that's going to get me anywhere in life.

—LORI GIARNELLA

Grandchildren

My grandchildren take me to the beach and try to make words out of the veins in my legs.

—PHYLLIS DILLER

I'm not even married yet and my future in-laws are already pressuring me to produce grandchildren. Their motto is "We're not losing a son, we're gaining a uterus."

—STEPHANIE SCHIERN

My mother wants grandchildren. I said, "Mom, go for it!"

—SUE MURPHY

Grandfathers

My grandfather is eighty-four and he's losing it. He gives advice that makes no sense, like, "It's a dog-eat-dog world. Just make sure your dog ain't anorexic."

—RENÉ HICKS

I remember my own dear grandfather. He smoked and drank every day of his life until he was eighty-one and we had to kill him.

—ROSEANNE BARR

Grandmothers

I cleaned out a cabinet that contained forty-eight years of greeting cards my grandma had gotten, and not one of them accurately reflected my grandmother. She needs her own line of cards like, "Grandma— Thanks for all the candles you lit for me when you thought I had a drinking problem."

—ELIZABETH BECKWITH

I never will forget my granny.... One day she's sitting out on the porch and I said, "Granny, how old does a woman get before she don't want no more boyfriends?" She was around 106 then. She said, "I don't know, honey, you'll have to ask somebody older than me."

—MOMS MABLEY

G-Spot

I can't find my G-spot. I don't understand; where is it? I logged on to MapQuest and everything. I'm beginning to think the G stands for "Gotcha, made you look."

—MARGARET CHO

I think the articles in women's magazines are totally unrealistic about what you can expect from a man in bed. I saw this article entitled "Training Your Man to Find Your G-spot." Get real. The guy I'm dating can't even find my apartment.

—LIVIA SQUIRES

I believe the only time it's appropriate for a man to go with the strong belief that he should not stop and ask for directions is when he's looking for my G-spot. No, you're not quite there yet, "Maybe veer to the left?" Oh, just keep going, you'll find it!

—NANCY PATTERSON

Guilt

My mother could make anybody feel guilty. She used to get letters of apology from people she didn't even know.

—JOAN RIVERS

When I miss my mom and her guilt trips, I watch PBS pledge breaks.

—BONNIE CHEESEMAN

Gun Control

The Second Amendment gave us the right to bear arms in order to have a ready militia. It's not for traffic incidents.

—PAULA POUNDSTONE

What's with the NRA? They don't want to outlaw automatic weapons. I guess you have to understand where they're coming from. They feel it's okay to shoot a human, as long as you eat the meat after.

—ELAYNE BOOSLER

Guns

This woman goes into a gun shop and says, "I want to buy a gun for my husband." The clerk asks, "Did he tell you what kind of gun?" "No," she replied, "he doesn't even know I'm going to shoot him."

—PHYLLIS DILLER

Gyms

There's this woman in my neighborhood who goes to the gym every single day. I see her in their window when I go out to get cigarettes.

—MICHELE BALAN

I never work out. I only go to the gym once a year, to renew. When I get the urge to exercise, I just lie down till it passes.

—LEMAIRE

My favorite machine at the gym is the vending machine.

—CAROLINE RHEA

My roommate is always bragging about her body. She's like, "I pay sixty bucks a month to the gym to get this." I told her, "Give me the money, I'll chase you around with a stick and we'll both lose weight."

—TRACEY MACDONALD

I worked out at this really fancy health club. They had a spiral StairMaster.

—WENDY LIEBMAN

Have you been to the gym lately? Boy, some of those guys overdevelop. If your neck is as wide as your head, take a day off.

—MARGARET SMITH

I really get irritated when guys try to hit on me at the gym by telling me how to use the equipment. I was working out with weights and this personal trainer asks, "Are you working on your biceps?" "No, I'm practicing my sledge hammer swings for my next serial kill."

—LISA MANNERKOSKI

I went to a gay gym; they were real gym rats. Guys are pressing forty bajillion pounds, women are pressing twice that. I look like I'm lifting a broomstick with two bagels on the end.

—SABRINA MATTHEWS

Gynecologists

It's an awkward situation. Did you ever want to ask your gynecologist, "Does your mother know what you do for a living?"

—JANE CONDON

It's silly for a woman to go to a male gynecologist. It's like going to an auto mechanic who has never owned a car.

—CARRIE SNOW

You know what ob-gyn means, don't you? It stands for "Ouch! Better groom your nails."

—JOAN RIVERS

At the gynecologist's they always ask, "What is the first day of your period?" I'm like, "I don't know, ask my dry cleaner."

—CAROL LEIFER

A pap smear is kinda like a throat culture, only you don't gag. Unless maybe if you're really short.

—SARAH SILVERSTEIN

The gynecologist says, "Relax, relax! You're not relaxed, I can't get my hand out." I wonder why I'm not relaxed? My feet are in the stirrups, my knees are in my face, and the door is open facing me.

—JOAN RIVERS

I went for my annual pap smear. Yeah, just one damn party after another. What I don't get is why doctors feel the need to explain everything they're doing during that exam. Do I ask for the gory details at Jiffy Lube? "This might feel a little cold," he explained. What he should have said was, "I'm now going to insert a frozen Otter Pop."

—SUSAN DEPHILLIPS

I got a postcard from my gynecologist. It said, "Did you know it's time for your annual checkup?" No. But now my mailman does. Why don't you just send me a petrie dish while you're at it?

—CATHY LADMAN

I had a wild year; I had my uterus yanked out. I had fibroids, but I didn't know it. My gynecologist said, "Suzanne, your uterus is really big." "Well, I've been working out."

—SUZANNE WESTENHOEFER

Hair

Nobody is really happy with what's on their head. People with straight hair want curly, people with curly want straight, and bald people want everyone to be blind.

—RITA RUDNER

I just had my hair cut. They cut my hair too short, and now I can't get it to do what I want it to. I want it to type.

—PAULA POUNDSTONE

I got a bad haircut recently. It was a haircut that actually redefined head trauma.

—CINDEE WEISS

I get a lot of clients with unreasonable expectations of what a hairdresser can accomplish. They want to look like *Friends,* and the closest I can get them is *Acquaintances.* Or maybe *Enemies.*

—LEMAIRE

I got my blonde hair from my mom. She bought me my first box of Nice 'n Easy.

—SANDI SELVI

Blondes have more fun, don't they? They must. How many brunettes do you see walking down the street with blonde roots?

—RITA RUDNER

I hate these women who lie about dyeing their hair. They tell men, "Oh, it was the sun. The sun turned my hair blonde." So how do you explain those black roots, honey? Did a cloud go by?

—TRACEY MACDONALD

I bleach my hair. No wonder my mind goes blank.

—BONNIE CHEESEMAN

I dye my hair so much, my driver's license has a color wheel.

—NANCY MURA

I found my first gray hair today. On my chest.

—WENDY LIEBMAN

It's too bad that when we age, our hair turns that awful gray color. It would be so much more pleasant to say, "I'm getting green around the temples," or "I've got a full head of purple hair."

—KELLY SMITH

I thought I looked good in the 1980s. I had big permed yellow hair, and it was permed, and big, and yellow. I thought I looked good, but in reality I was the Lion King.

—SHAWN PELOFSKY

In the '70s women used to iron their hair. I tried it once, but I burnt the hell out of my thighs.

—DEBBIE KASPER

I refuse to think of them as chin hairs. I like to think of them as stray eyebrows.

—JANETTE BARBER

If I don't tweeze every day, my eyebrows need barrettes.

—NANCY MURA

Happiness

Happiness is finding a book that's three weeks overdue, and you're not.

—TOTIE FIELDS

Sometimes when I'm happy I feel just like crying, but when I'm sad I never feel like laughing. So I think it's better to be happy; you can get two feelings for the price of one.

—LILY TOMLIN

Harassment

Yet another obnoxious attempt by men to try to get your attention: They hiss. "Sssss! Sssss!" But I like to think of it as the sound of their ego deflating as I continue to walk away.

—MIMI GONZALEZ

I hate when I have to walk down the street past construction workers and they always say something disgusting. It wouldn't bother me so much if they could show me even one marriage that came from this kind of introduction. "Mommy, how did you meet Daddy?" "Well, I was walking along the street one day, and your father screamed something about wanting to eat his lunch off my ass. I was so turned on, I threw myself in the back of his truck."

—CAROLINE RHEA

I really hate it when strange men on the street say, "Smile! You'd look so much prettier if you'd smile." I always feel like saying, "Get hard! You'd look so much more useful if you had an erection."

—CATHRYN MICHON

I quit a job once because of sexual harassment. There was nowhere near enough of it going on to keep me around. I got needs.

—MEL FINE

Sexual harassment at work, is it a problem for the self-employed?

—VICTORIA WOOD

Health Supplements

I take geranium, dandelion, passionflower, hibiscus. I feel great, and when I pee, I experience the fresh scent of potpourri.

—SHEILA WENZ

How do vitamins know where to go? A is supposed to help the eyes, E the heart; do they have a map? I take them, but I don't feel better. But I guess when you take your vitamins with vodka, they get tipsy and confused, lose the map and go straight to my breasts. Like most guys after a couple drinks.

—JAYNE WARREN

I take vitamins. They drop and roll under the refrigerator. I don't pick them up. I have years of vitamins under the refrigerator. I'm going to come home one night and find a six-foot roach saying, "I feel good!"

—ELAYNE BOOSLER

Height

Short guys are always saying stupid things to me because I'm so tall. One guy asked, "Do you play basketball?" I said, "No, do you play miniature golf?"

—FRANCES DILORINZO

I like to date short guys because us women love anything we can throw into our purse. "Let's see, keys, lipstick—oh, I forgot I was dating you, and you've eaten all my Altoids."

—LEMAIRE

Being a tall woman, I always dated guys for their height rather than their wealth, because I wasn't thinking.

—FRANCES DILORINZO

Hell

Most major religions use hell as a deterrent to bad activity. But I find the concept of hell quite comforting because, hey, at least I'll know people there.

—MARGOT BLACK

I think hell will be whatever your mind's-eye idea of hell is. Unfortunately, I've come face-to-face with what mine will be: I'm going to be sentenced to the StairMaster ring of Dante's Inferno. And StairMaster time is the slowest increment of time known to man. And the only music I'll get is Michael Bolton, karaoke-style from a drunken secretary on Margarita Night.

—JANEANE GAROFALO

Heterosexuals

I was raised around heterosexuals. That's where us gay people come from: you heterosexuals.

—ELLEN DEGENERES

Hobbies

I've been working out lately. It's my new hobby. I thought I already had a hobby, but apparently going out, getting stinking drunk, and giving creepy guys phony phone numbers is not actually considered a hobby, but a "lifestyle."

—ANDI RHOADS

Holidays

I love real holidays, not this made-up stuff. But every month apparently has to have a theme. Like October is Breast Awareness Month. Did we need to be reminded? I've been aware of mine since I was eleven. We grew up together . . . bosom buddies.

—LEE ARLETH

I'm still keeping my New Year's resolutions. I actually only make one because it's the only one easy to keep: I resolve to spend less time with my family.

—MARIA MENOZZI

This year, for my New Year's resolution I joined a gym. Next year my resolution is to start going.

—DAVA KRAUSE

Valentine's Day blows. It's just another day for you to wake up late, wonder how you're going to pay rent, spend the day sulking in your underwear and a cute T-shirt, eat a Goober grape sandwich, and half-assedly clean your apartment. Did I say "you"? Sorry, I meant me.

—JESSICA DELFINO

G. H. 7

I have the same New Year's resolution every year: I decide to drink heavily. Because I know I can do it, which will build my self-esteem.

—BETSY SALKIND

Here would be my Valentine's card that I think I'm gonna send to my boyfriend: "Things have been going so well thus far, I will find more ways to become unavailable to you."

—JANEANE GAROFALO

Valentine's is a big day for married people. A lot of anticipation. One of the three days you get laid: Valentine's Day, Christmas, your birthday—maybe.

—AISHA TYLER

I wanted to make it really special on Valentine's Day, so I tied my boyfriend up. And for three solid hours I watched whatever I wanted to on TV.

—TRACY SMITH

My mom wanted to know why I never get home for the holidays. I said, "Because I can't get Delta to wait in the yard while I run in."

—MARGARET SMITH

When I was little I asked my mother, "Do you love me?" She said, "I love you when you're sleeping." When I was fourteen, I asked, "Mom, am I ugly?" She said, "It's okay, when you're sixteen you can get a nose job." When I was leaving for school, she said, "I don't know why we're spending any money to send you to college—you don't deserve it." When I came home for Mother's Day, she asked, "Where is my present?" I said, "Your present is, I still only have one personality and it's not planning to kill you!"

—ROBIN ROBERTS

When I was twelve I went as my mother for Halloween. I put on a pair of heels, went door to door, and criticized what everyone else was wearing.

—ROBIN BACH

Halloween was confusing. All my life my parents said, "Never take candy from strangers." And then they dressed me up and said, "Go beg for it." I didn't know what to do. I'd knock on people's doors, and go, "Trick or treat. No thank you."

—RITA RUDNER

In Wal-Mart I saw a sign advertising a "turkey hunting clinic." So what do they do, show you how to dress warm and sneak up real quiet and *snatch* them from the freezer case?

—VICKI TREMBLY

Thanksgiving morning, at my parents' house: "I can't believe you drank the last of the vodka! Now how the hell am I going to baste the turkey?"

—KELLI DUNHAM

I'm Jewish and I got a little annoyed this Christmas because the kids next door tried to sell me Bible calendars, and then church candies, and then this little inchlong baby Jesus in a crèche. I finally gave in. "Sure, I'd love to buy your Baby Jesus in a box." But I figured I'd pay them with Hanukkah gelt. "Is that one, or two, chocolate doubloons for the Lord Savior of the world?"

—JENNIFER POST

I was an elf for the mall Santa. Turns out nothing can get you out of the Christmas spirit quite like children. One lollipop stuck in your hair, and you find yourself saying, "This year for Christmas, Santa is bringing you a big box of *death*."

—KRIS MCGAHA

Probably the worst thing about being Jewish during Christmastime is shopping, because the lines are so long. They should have a Jewish express line: "Look, I'm a Jew, it's not a gift. It's just paper towels!"

—SUE KOLINSKY

It took me three weeks to stuff the turkey. I stuffed it through the beak.

—PHYLLIS DILLER

What I don't like about office Christmas parties is looking for a job the next day.

—PHYLLIS DILLER

On Christmas Eve my father would have 182 beers and then put our bikes together. "Oh, look, there are handlebars on my stereo. Why don't you have another highball and put some brakes on the dining room table with all those bolts you have left over?"

—KATHLEEN MADIGAN

My husband is so cheap, on Christmas Eve he fires one shot and tells the kids Santa committed suicide.

—PHYLLIS DILLER

Home Décor

I'd never heard the term *feng shui* until I moved to Los Angeles. Apparently, it involves someone rearranging your home and creating open spaces so as to adjust the energy in your life. We have something similar to that in Oklahoma; it's called burglary.

—C. LYNN MITCHELL

I have French doors in the bedroom. They don't open unless I lick them.

—JUDY GOLD

Homelessness

I always give homeless people money, and my friends yell at me, "He's only going to buy more alcohol and cigarettes." And I'm thinking, "Oh, like I wasn't?"

—KATHLEEN MADIGAN

Homosexuality

As women, as lesbians and gay men, we are denied certain very basic human rights. The last time most people in this society cared about my rights, I was a fetus. And the next time they'll care about my rights is when I die and come back as a whale.

—SARA CYTRON

When I first came out to my family they shunned me. You know, when I think back to that time, I kind of liked it.

—KATE CLINTON

The heterosexuals who hate us should just stop having us.

—LYNDA MONTGOMERY

I had a hard time telling my parents I'm gay, so I broke the news to them gradually: I told them I wasn't gay, but the woman I was sleeping with was.

—E. L. GREGGORY

Here is a little tip for all of you. Don't come out to your father in a moving vehicle.

—KATE CLINTON

I'm out for everybody in my family, except for my aunt. She's agoraphobic, and I figure if she won't come out for me, why should I come out for her?

—LYNDA MONTGOMERY

When my parents would first come and visit I would go through the whole "de-dyking" of the apartment. We call it straightening up.

—KATE CLINTON

My grandmother actually knew I was gay before I did. I really didn't know. My grandmother turned to me, in her Yiddish accent, she says, "So, Judy, what? Are you a homosectional?" I thought that was something you bought in department stores, "I'd like two end tables, and that lovely homosectional."

—JUDY CARTER

My brother is gay and my parents don't care, as long as he marries a doctor.

—ELAYNE BOOSLER

I always tell people I'm queer right away. Because if you're really smart about it, you can get the whole row on the plane. "I swear to God, sir, I'm a lesbian. If you don't move, I'll touch your wife during the movie."

—SUZANNE WESTENHOEFER

I love my gay male friends so much. When I was a little girl I always wished that I would be constantly surrounded by gorgeous men, and now I am. I should have been more specific.

—MARGARET CHO

I thank God for creating gay men. Because if it wasn't for them, us fat women would have no one to dance with.

—ROSEANNE BARR

Gay Republicans, how exactly does that work? "We disapprove of our own lifestyle. We beat ourselves up in parking lots."

—PAULA POUNDSTONE

Lots of people think that bisexual means cowardly lesbian.

—SANDRA BERNHARD

Straight people are afraid of us. I had a woman totally flip out on me when she found out I was a lesbian. "Oh my God. Now that I know you're a lesbian, I can't get undressed in front of you." I'm like, "Really, miss, just take my order."

—SUZANNE WESTENHOEFER

I was performing at a comedy club and when I said I'm a lesbian, a guy in the audience yelled out, "Can I watch?" I said, "Watch me what? Fix my car?"

—SABRINA MATTHEWS

There are a lot of places that gay people don't fit in. Like Sears.

—SUZANNE WESTENHOEFER

If all gay people are going to hell, I'd like to see everyone in heaven get their hair done.

—JUDY CARTER

My girlfriend and I want the right to have a legal wedding, but we don't want to get married. We're queer, not crazy.

—MARGA GOMEZ

If homosexuality is a disease, let's all call in queer to work. "Hello, can't work today. Still queer."

—ROBIN TYLER

The next time someone asks you, "Hey, how did you get to be a homosexual anyway?" tell them, "Homosexuals are chosen first on talent, then interview. The swimsuit and evening gown competition pretty much gets rid of the rest of them."

—KAREN WILLIAMS

My boyfriend and I saw two guys holding hands, and he completely freaked. "That's gross! I'd never do anything like that. That's immoral." But if I were to show him a picture of two naked women together, this is how he thinks, "What's missing? *Me!*"

—FELICIA MICHAELS

Housekeeping

I'm a lazy housekeeper. I run out of toilet paper, I use tissues, run out of tissues, I use cotton balls. You're just not my friend until you've been in my house, on the way to the bathroom, and I can turn to you and say, "Here, take a coffee filter."

—MARGOT BLACK

Housewives

I'm a housewife, but I prefer to be called a domestic goddess.

—ROSEANNE BARR

Housework

Living together, it's like I'm a prostitute for really low wages. "I'll do oral and anal, if you take out the garbage."

—MARGARET CHO

Housework can't kill you, but why take a chance?

—PHYLLIS DILLER

I was taking caring of myself before I got married; my husband was taking care of himself. I thought, let's just continue down this path. But he would come home and say stuff to me that I just didn't understand. Like, "What's for dinner?" I reply, "I don't know. What did you cook?" And he actually said this one time, "I'm all out of clean underwear." To which I replied, "Ooh, then you need to wash. I did my laundry yesterday, I got a drawer full of clean panties. You're welcome to borrow a pair to tide you over."

—WANDA SYKES

I'm not the least bit domestic, and I don't care. We have a ring around the tub you could set a drink on.

—PHYLLIS DILLER

I never get tired of housework. I don't do any. When guests come to visit, I just put out dropcloths and say we're painting.

—JOAN RIVERS

My mother used to say, "You can eat off my floor." You can eat off my floor, too. There are thousands of things there.

—ELAYNE BOOSLER

Sometimes I can be a real slob. I once walked into my house and thought, "Oh no, I've been robbed!" And then I realized I'd left it that way.

—MARGOT BLACK

My daughter is a typical teen. Her room is so gross, cockroaches put on combat boots before they'll walk in there.

—SHEILA KAY

I love it when my husband thinks I might leave him. He gets so insecure, he does the dishes. But I'd have to file divorce papers to get him to clean the toilet.

—SHIRLEY LIPNER

Don't cook. Don't clean. No man will ever make love to a woman because she waxed the linoleum. "My God, the floor's immaculate. Lie down, you hot bitch."

—JOAN RIVERS

My ex-husband cheated on me, even though I was a good wife and mother; I cleaned, I cooked. The way to a man's heart may be through his stomach, but that's only if you twist the blade and lift up.

—SHEILA KAY

Cleaning the house before your kids are done growing is like shoveling the walk before it stops snowing.

—PHYLLIS DILLER

You never hear a kid say, "I should probably Scotchgard that."

—ELLEN DEGENERES

You make the beds, you do the dishes, and six months later you have to start all over again.

—JOAN RIVERS

I buried a lot of my ironing in the backyard.

—PHYLLIS DILLER

I do clean up a little. If company is coming, I'll wipe the lipstick off the milk container.

—ELAYNE BOOSLER

Last year I left my job to stay home with my kids. One nice thing about it is, I'm my own boss. So I declared Real Casual Fridays. I don't get out of bed.

—EILEEN COURTNEY

So I live in this apartment that's disgusting; it's really dirty. And the kitchen floor is, like, sticky. I had to do something about it, so finally I went out and bought some slippers.

—SARAH SILVERMAN

It is better to light just one candle than to clean the whole apartment.

—EILEEN COURTNEY

Humanity

I think I'm a pretty good judge of people, which is why I hate most of them.

—ROSEANNE BARR

Aren't people stupid? Not us, it's the others. Ever notice that when you're with someone and they taste something bad, they want you to taste it, too? "This is disgusting! It's gross! Taste this, taste how bad it is!" And we're stupid, we taste it. "All right. I'm going to vomit!"

—ELLEN DEGENERES

I hate people. People make me pro-nuclear.

—MARGARET SMITH

Humor

Men always say the most important thing in a woman is a sense of humor. You know what that means? He's looking for someone to laugh at *his* jokes.

—SHEILA WENZ

Hunting

You ask people why they have deer heads on the wall. They say, "Because it's such a beautiful animal." I think my mother's attractive, but I have photographs of her.

—ELLEN DEGENERES

Husbands

I want to get married but I look at husbands the same way I look at tattoos. I want one, but I can't decide what I want, and I don't want to be stuck with something I'd grow to hate and have surgically removed. Why can't I just have a henna husband?

—MARGARET CHO

When I get married, I want a regular husband. I don't want a soul mate, because eventually husbands and wives start to hate each other. And when you think about it, a husband is only until "death do you part." But a soul mate is going to harass you for all eternity.

—LIVIA SQUIRES

He tricked me into marrying him. He told me he was pregnant.

—CAROL LEIFER

My husband and I are totally different. My friends always try to make me feel better by saying "opposites attract." I guess that's true because he was a virgin, and I . . .

—FRANCES DILORINZO

My husband says, "Roseanne, don't you think we ought to talk about our sexual problems?" Like I'm gonna turn off *Wheel of Fortune* for that.

—ROSEANNE BARR

I want my husband to take me in his arms and whisper those three little words that all women long to hear: "You were right."

—KELLY SMITH

Trust your husband, adore your husband, and get as much as you can in your own name.

—JOAN RIVERS

My husband and I used to fight about that night out with the guys, but it's not like I was doing it every night.

—JENNY JONES

When you want your husband to play with you, wear a full-length black nightgown with buttons all over it. Sure, it's uncomfortable, but it makes you look just like his remote control.

—DIANA JORDAN

When I was sixteen years old, I dated my husband for about a month, before I dumped him. Then when I was eighteen, I dated him again for three months before I broke up with him, because I thought it wasn't going anywhere. When I was twenty-eight, I married him. I was thinking, "If I dump him this time, I get to keep his stuff."

—FRANCES DILORINZO

The only thing my husband and I have in common is that we were married on the same day.

—PHYLLIS DILLER

They think it's your destiny to clean, and I guess it's their destiny to have a couch surgically implanted on their behind. You may marry the man of your dreams, ladies, but years later you're married to a couch that burps.

—ROSEANNE BARR

Does your husband sit around the house in his shorts, fart and drink beer, and watch football? All right! I do that, too. My new husband tells me that's not very ladylike. I say, "Neither is a blow job, and you don't complain about that." Which pretty much ends that conversation.

—DIANE FORD

My husband was an animal in bed. A ferret.

—WENDY LIEBMAN

My husband is so quiet, I've collected life insurance on him twice.

—JEAN CARROLL

I've been asked to say a couple of words about my husband, Fang. How about "short" and "cheap"?

—PHYLLIS DILLER

Husbands think we should know where everything is, like the uterus is a tracking device. He asks me, "Roseanne, do we have any Chee-tos left?" Like he can't go over to that sofa cushion and lift it himself.

—ROSEANNE BARR

He was cheating on me with his secretary. I found lipstick on his collar, covered with Wite-Out.

—WENDY LIEBMAN

My husband was so ugly he hurt my feelings. He had a job in a doctor's office standing by the door making people sick.

—MOMS MABLEY

My husband said he needed more space. So I locked him outside.

—ROSEANNE BARR

Hypochondria

I worry that I worry too much. I think I got the only illness *not* covered by health insurance: hypochondria. My dozen doctors can't be wrong. But what am I going to do, take placebos? They're probably addicting, and you can't buy them on the street. I don't want to be breaking into science labs, stealing control placebos from mice.

—JAYNE WARREN

Immigration

Pat Buchanan suggested that illegal immigration be stopped by building a wall around America. I bet the Indians wished they'd thought of that first.

—LEIGHANN LORD

Inconsideration

I'm getting more and more inconsiderate. I slept with a young guy and afterward I said, "That was fun. It's been so long since I've slept with someone for a ride home."

—LAURA KIGHTLINGER

Ineptitude

We all feel like idiots at one time or another. Even if we feel we're cool 98 percent of the time, that 2 percent doofus is poised to take over our bodies without any warning. It just takes a crack in the sidewalk, one little trip. We feel like fools, turning back to look at it. "There's a pebble, somebody better put up some orange cones to warn others. Everybody's gonna trip like I did." Then we look back that one more time to show the pebble who's boss, "Damn pebble, why-I-oughta . . ."

—ELLEN DEGENERES

In-laws

My mother-in-law finally died. For the twenty-one years of my marriage she always referred to me as "Edgar's first wife."

—JOAN RIVERS

Insects

I'd like to be a fish fly. It's a bug that only lives one day. That's right, they're born, they mate, they die. Kinda takes all the worry out of "Will he ever call me again?"

—LISA GOICH

Ever watch ants just crawling around? They walk in that single straight line, a long, long mile of ants. Sometimes they will walk over and pick up their dead friends and carry those around. I'm pretty sure it's because they can get in the carpool lane and pass up that line.

—ELLEN DEGENERES

I was reading how a female spider will eat the male spider after mating. I guess female spiders know that life insurance is easier to collect than child support.

—JANINE DITULLIO

Butterflies live an average of fourteen to twenty-one days. About the same time it takes to get a mail-in rebate.

—ELLEN DEGENERES

Insomnia

I use poor man's psychotherapy: insomnia. Where I lay awake trying to figure out what's wrong with me. Or if anything's *not* wrong with me.

—JAYNE WARREN

I can't sleep. I have insomnia. I had a nightmare last night. I dreamt my parents came to visit . . . that's it.

—CATHY LADMAN

Insurance

My late husband was so old he got out of breath trying to thread a needle. I told him, "Honey, you're sick. Why don't you take out some insurance?" He said, "I ain't gonna take out a damn bit. When I die I want it to be a sad day for everybody."

—MOMS MABLEY

Integrity

You're only a sellout if you had any integrity to begin with.

—MEL FINE

Truth is, I've always been selling out. The difference is that in the past, I looked like I had integrity because there were no buyers.

—LILY TOMLIN

Internet

I read an article the other day that said more and more bosses are becoming aware of their employees' need for Internet access. I don't believe that. Has anybody, anywhere, in any office actually seen somebody who is doing work on the Internet? Get real. Half the people in my office are on there looking for other jobs.

—LIVIA SQUIRES

If you have friends addicted to eBay, intervene quick. One minute they're spending a few bucks a month on kitschy collectibles, the next thing the site becomes their only contact with the outside world. Two weeks later you call, "Hey, why aren't you at work?" "I'm in a bidding war over a six-pack of Diet Coke!"

—KELLI DUNHAM

I have so much cyber sex, my baby's first words will be "You've got mail."

—PAULARA R. HAWKINS

Introductions

The way someone is introduced tells you a lot about where he stands in a relationship. Like, "This is my friend," means "He's not touching me." "This is my boyfriend," means, "We're doing it all the time." "This is my husband," means, "He's not touching me." "This is my agent," means, "We're doing it all the time."

—FRANCES DILORINZO

Introductions are tricky in a lesbian relationship. It's a word game. To my friends she's my lover, to strangers and family members in denial she's my roommate, to Jehovah's Witnesses at the door she's my lesbian sex slave, and to my mother she's Jewish and that's all that matters.

—DENISE MCCANLES

Inventions

The people who invented nonalcoholic beer are working on liver without vitamins.

—ELAYNE BOOSLER

I don't know if I want a fuzzy cover on my toilet seat, but I want to meet whoever invented them. Who lifted a toilet seat and thought, "That needs a hat."

—RITA RUDNER

Irony

Irony. Is that when you put on a brand-new exercise outfit and then spend the rest of the day watching the Olympics?

—SIMONE ALEXANDER

Jealousy

I'm very, very jealous. Sometimes I walk down the street and I see a beautiful woman and I think to myself, "I'll bet my boyfriend would like to sleep with her," and I get so angry. I run right home and smack him, and say, "*How much more of this do you think I can take?*"

—DENISE MUNRO ROBB

Job Interviews

It's so humiliating to go on job interviews, especially when they ask, "What was the reason you left your last job?" "Well, I found that after I was fired there was a lot of tension in the office. You know, I found it difficult sitting on the new girl's lap."

—CAROLINE RHEA

When I was applying for a job I went from having no discernible skills to lying about having no discernible skills.

—MAUREEN BROWNSEY

Jobs

I got my first full-time job, but it's weird. I could have sworn I was making more money in college, working for my parents as their daughter.

—MELANIE RENO

I had the most boring office job in the world. I used to clean the windows on envelopes.

—RITA RUDNER

I have one of those 24/7 jobs: I'm a divorced mom with no alimony.

—SULLY DIAZ

I got this office job as someone's assistant. Which basically means I'm their bitch.

—MELANIE RENO

One time I tried getting a job at a submarine-sandwich shop, only they wanted me to take a lie detector test just in order to apply for the job. What the hell am I going to lie about in a sub shop? Did they fear someone would ask for roast beef and I'd say no? "How much is the tuna?" "Thousands."

—PAULA POUNDSTONE

The weirdest job I ever had was in sales for wholesale beef. Very bizarre job, because I'm a vegetarian. But I figured, if a priest can be a marriage counselor, I can sell some beef.

—DIANE NICHOLS

I was a stewardess for a while on a helicopter. For about five or six people, tops. I'd ask, "Would you like something to drink? You would? Then we're going to have to land."

—RITA RUDNER

I sold cemetery plots for seven years. My ex-mother-in-law was always criticizing me. So I promised her a family discount if she would drop dead.

—SONYA SHARPSHIRE

Jury Duty

Juries scare me. I don't want to put my fate in the hands of twelve people who couldn't get out of jury duty.

—MONICA PIPER

My mother is a typical Jewish mother. They sent her home from jury duty. She insisted *she* was guilty.

—CATHY LADMAN

Kids

It would seem that something which means poverty, disorder, and violence every single day should be avoided entirely, but the desire to beget children is a natural urge.

—PHYLLIS DILLER

Why do I want a child? Does giving birth make me a real woman? No, earning less than a man makes me a real woman.

—SUZY BERGER

I was visiting my brother earlier today, and he's childproofing his home. I don't understand that. He even put little rubber bumpers on the sharp edges, like the table tops and everything, little bumpers, so now you go over there and the kids just run around all day. So what I do, I'm walking around, I sneak around, I slip those little bumpers off. And then I give the kids candy. "Why don't you all sit down for a minute." They don't listen. They turn one of those corners. Bam! You see, stitches will slow you down, won't it?

—WANDA SYKES

I think about having children, because time is running out. I want to have children while my parents are still young enough to take care of them.

—RITA RUDNER

I remember when I first got my foster son. He was the cutest little guy I'd seen in my life. I always knew that I'd be responsible. As I changed him, I was surprised by how much I liked it. I knew that I'd do what needed to be done. But there was always that little voice in the back of my head that said, "Remember, the saxophone was in the closet after a month."

—PAULA POUNDSTONE

You never know what you're going to get, and children have their own personalities immediately. I was watching little kids on a carousel: Some kids were jumping on the horses, some kids were afraid of the horses, some kids were betting on the horses.

—RITA RUDNER

We spend the first twelve months of our children's lives teaching them to walk and talk and the next twelve telling them to sit down and shut up.

—PHYLLIS DILLER

A child of one can be taught not to do certain things, such as touch a hot stove, pull lamps off of tables, and wake Mommy before noon.

—JOAN RIVERS

I'm forty-three, and I have a two-year-old. And I did it on purpose, so you know I'm not that bright.

—STEPHANIE HODGE

Have you ever had a four-year-old tell you a joke? It takes about two hours, has no semblance of order, and you have to know when it's over.

—ROSIE O'DONNELL

My son is into that nose-picking thing. The least he can do is act like an adult: Buy a car and sit in traffic.

—ROSEANNE BARR

What's harder to raise, boys or girls? Girls. Boys are easy. Give 'em a book of matches and they're happy.

—ETTA MAY

Most children threaten at times to run away from home. This is the only thing that keeps some parents going.

—PHYLLIS DILLER

I've been married fourteen years and I have three kids. Obviously, I breed well in captivity.

—ROSEANNE BARR

Always be nice to your children, because they are the ones who will choose your rest home.

—PHYLLIS DILLER

I'm afraid to have children because what if they turned out to have bad personalities? I'd have to take them places and be like, "Yeah, these are my kids. And they're so not cool."

—SARI KARPLUS

I can't have children. Because I have white couches.

—CARRIE SNOW

The only real joy I'm having in not having any children is that it's driving my parents crazy, and I really like that a lot. I feel like I'm getting even for all those years in high school when they made me come home early and I couldn't have sex.

—ELAYNE BOOSLER

I'm not a breeder. I have no maternal instincts whatsoever. I ovulate sand.

—MARGARET CHO

We've been married six years, so people are trying to force us to have kids. They all say the same thing, "Kids, they a lot of work, but they worth it." But I noticed something: They never look you in the eye when they say that.

—WANDA SYKES

I would like to have kids one day, but I only have one egg left. Uh-oh, there it went, sorry. I'm ovulating right now.

—CATHY LADMAN

I don't have any kids. Well, at least none I know about.

—CAROL LEIFER

We've begun to long for the pitter-patter of little feet, so we bought a dog. Well, it's cheaper, and you get more feet.

—RITA RUDNER

At the mall I saw a kid on a leash. And I think if I ever have a kid, it's gonna be cordless.

—WENDY LIEBMAN

Kids? It's like living with homeless people. They're cute but they just chase you around all day long going, "Can I have a dollar? I'm missing a shoe! I need a ride!"

—KATHLEEN MADIGAN

I have a kid from my first marriage, because I like souvenirs.

—CORY KAHANEY

Having kids around the house I realize the stupid things I say to them that my parents used to say to me. Like, "Stop making faces or you'll stay that way." I remember looking at one of my uncles thinking, "So *that's* what happened to him."

—MARIA MENOZZI

The way we know the kids are growing up: The bite marks are higher.

—PHYLLIS DILLER

Kids are cute, babies are cute, puppies are cute. The little things are cute. See, nature did this on purpose so that we would want to take care of our young. Made them cute. Tricked us. Then gradually they get older and older, until one day your mother sits you down and says, "You know, I think you're ugly enough to get your own apartment."

—CATHY LADMAN

Kids are cute, but they're so rude. I was taking a shower when my daughter came in and said, "Gosh, Mom, I hope when I grow up my breasts are nice and long like yours."

—ROSEANNE BARR

Kids love me, they love my stories. Like "Sparky, the Bathtub Toaster."

—SHARI BECKER

You never hear a kid say, "Do you want me to dust the baseboards?"

—ELLEN DEGENERES

Laundry

I hate doing laundry. I don't separate the colors from the whites. I put them together and let them learn from their cultural differences.

—RITA RUDNER

Have you noticed that if you leave laundry in the hamper long enough, it's ready to wear again?

—ELAYNE BOOSLER

Lawsuits

Did you hear about that woman who got paid $3 million for spilling hot coffee on her crotch at McDonald's? Three million dollars! I wish someone had given me that opportunity, before I wasted all that time in college. If they had just laid it all out for me: "Okay, you can spend four to five years at a local university, graduate, and earn maybe $30,000 a year, working every single day for the rest of your life. Or, scalding hot java in your cooch: 3 million!" I'd be like, "Could that be decaf? I get irritable."

—ROBIN GREENSPAN

Lazy

How do lazy people work up the motivation to procrastinate?

—ELLEN DEGENERES

I'm lazy. At work my favorite part of the day is being on hold.

—JANET ROSEN

I'm the laziest person. I know I'm not supposed to admit that because—
wooo, the work ethic! We lazy slobs get such a bad rap, but you people
should be thanking us. Because if it weren't for us lazy bastards, you
guys wouldn't have gotten into college.

—ANN OELSCHLAGER

Lesbians

You know, my family always said no man would be good enough for me.

—SUZY BERGER

My five-year-old nephew asked his mother, "Can two women have a
baby?" She told him, "No." Then my nephew said, "But they can try, right?"

—KATE CLINTON

Being gay or lesbian is not a "lifestyle." Disco was a lifestyle. Being gay or
lesbian is about our lives, about affectional preference, about our right
to love. If I never had sex with another woman again, I would still be a
lesbian. I wouldn't be a very happy lesbian, but I would still be a lesbian.

—ROBIN TYLER

Heterosexuals are rude sometimes, get right in your face and ask you rude questions, "What do you lesbians do in bed?" Well, it's a lot like heterosexual sex. Only, one of us doesn't have to fake an orgasm.

—SUZANNE WESTENHOEFER

People think you're a lesbian because you can't get a man. Then explain to me why the only times in my life I've slept with men was when I couldn't get a woman?

—GEORGIA RAGSDALE

One man asked, "Hey, did you get that way because you had some kind of bad sexual experience with a guy?" I'm like, "If that's all it took, the entire female population would be gay, sir."

—SUZANNE WESTENHOEFER

It's not that I don't like penises. I just don't like them on men.

—LEA DELARIA

That word *lesbian* sounds like a disease. And straight men know, because they're sure that they're the cure.

—DENISE MCCANLES

I recently got an invitation to a dinner party. It said: "Please let us know if you have any dietary restrictions." I replied, "Yes, I only eat women."

—JENNIFER POST

Some women can't say the word *lesbian,* even when their mouth is full of one.

—KATE CLINTON

A lot of lesbians are vegetarians. They say they won't eat anything that has a face. So what do they do in bed?

—JENNIFER POST

The most terrifying commandment I ever heard was good old number nine: Thou shalt not covet thy neighbor's wife. I heard that commandment and I thought it had my name on it.

—KATE CLINTON

My mother always told me, "Marry someone like your father." I knew I was a dyke, but to this day I'm so set on pleasing my mother that I now find myself attracted to women who are balding and have a beer belly.

—MONICA GRANT

Who writes the titles under the heads on those talk shows? Every time a fierce, fabulous, Amazonian-looking babe appears there's a title under her head that says, "Lesbian who hates men." Like we have time.

—KATE CLINTON

They say that lesbians hate men. Why would a lesbian hate a man? They don't have to fuck them.

—ROSEANNE BARR

It's hard to be a lesbian comedian these days. "These days," like there was an easier time. Oh, the Renaissance, that was a good time to be a lesbian comedian.

—KATE CLINTON

I'm not a lesbian. Which is a shame, because I'm so good at softball.

—MARGARET CHO

I'm in couples therapy. I'm now doing things I always made fun of. Except guys, of course.

—KATE CLINTON

License Plates

My license plate says PMS. Nobody cuts me off.

—WENDY LIEBMAN

Life

I think life is perverse. It can be beautiful, but it won't.

—LILY TOMLIN

The best things in life really are free. So, how many kittens do you want?

—NANCY JO PERDUE

Life is like a game of poker: If you don't put any in the pot, there won't be any to take out.

—MOMS MABLEY

Life isn't fair. My husband's birthday is October 9. When it falls on a Monday, it's Columbus Day, a holiday. My birthday is April 17. When it falls on Monday, it's tax day. My thirtieth birthday fell on Monday, it was tax day, raining, and I was pregnant. If you throw in a dog and a pickup truck, you've got all the makings of a country song.

—SHANNON IRELAND

Do you ever feel that your life is like an Etch a Sketch? You know where you wanna go, but darned if you can figure out how to get there.

—KATE CLINTON

If I've learned one thing in life, it's that I can always count on pinkeye at the most inappropriate moment.

—JANEANE GAROFALO

You've got to be happy with your life, with what you do. Because if you're not, you have to go on a talk show and tell everybody about it.

—LAURA KIGHTLINGER

Life, death. If I could do it all over again, I wouldn't use Nair on my upper lip.

—BETH DAVIDOFF

I'm in love with life, but talk about the possibility of a bad breakup.

—CHRISTINA IRENE

Lines

The greatest line I ever heard was from this guy who said, "I like a woman who can give me a real challenge." So I mailed him my bank statement. Figure this out, big guy.

—DIANE NICHOLS

Guys I've been meeting have the worst pickup lines. Like, "Hey, what's your friend's name?"

—MELANIE RENO

A guy came up to me in a bar and said, "I'm so good in bed, after we make love you won't be able to walk." I'm thinking, "Is that a good thing?" I mean, I want to get laid, but I don't want to be a cripple.

—LIVIA SQUIRES

The men are so rude, especially the lines they come up with. For example, if a man tells you he likes to go for long walks, it means he doesn't own a car. If he says he enjoys romantic dinners at home, it means he's broke.

—PAULA BELL

I hate bars. Guys come up to me and say, "Hey, cupcake, can I buy you a drink?" I say, "No, but I'll take the six bucks."

—MARGARET SMITH

This guy I met in a bar said, "When I make love I turn into an animal." Well, that's a step up.

—JUDY TENUTA

At the end of the date this guy pulled out the oldest line, "Hey, baby how about breakfast? Should I call you, or nudge you?" I said, "Write me."

—DIANE NICHOLS

I love the lines the men use to get us into bed. "Please, I'll only put it in for a minute." What am I, a microwave?

—BEVERLY MICKINS

Liquor

They've put warning labels on liquor. "Caution: Alcohol can be dangerous to pregnant women." Did you read that? That's ironic. If it weren't for alcohol, most women would never be that way.

—RITA RUDNER

Living Will

People who do not want to be resuscitated now have the option to wear a bracelet that says DO NOT RESUSCITATE. To me this sounds like a great gift for someone you hate. What if you put the wrong bracelet on one night? You're out having dinner, you pass out, and twenty minutes later you're in the morgue. And all you wanted to do was accessorize.

—JOY BEHAR

Looks

I always get passed up for the kind of girls with the blue eyes and the blond hair, who go to the mall and actually buy stuff. You know, the ones with the manicures and pedicures, who shower every day. And I'm busy, dude.

—COURTNEY CRONIN

I'm not picky. I just want to meet someone I'd like to be with both in the bedroom and in public. But if you're looking for that special someone in a bar, ladies, please remember that there are reasons bars are dark.

—LYNN EPSTEIN

There are a lot of good-looking men out there. But keep in mind that no matter how cute and sexy a guy is, there's always some woman somewhere who is sick of him.

—CAROL HENRY

Love

You know you're in love when you're willing to share your cash-machine number.

—ELAYNE BOOSLER

Before I met my husband I'd never fallen in love, though I've stepped in it a few times.

—RITA RUDNER

If you open your heart up and let all the love you have flow out of you, I promise that some highly dysfunctional, emotionally unavailable man will glom himself onto you and never let go.

—WENDY KAMENOFF

I urge you all to love yourselves without reservation, and to love each other without restraints. Unless you're into leather. Then, by all means, use restraints.

—MARGARET CHO

Don't you hate it when you date someone and they say this: "I love you, but I'm not in love with you." You just want to go, "I want you, but not inside me."

—FELICIA MICHAELS

I fall in love really quickly and this scares guys away. I'm like, "I'm in love with you, I want to marry you, I want to move in with you." And they're like, "Ma'am, could you give me the ten bucks for the pizza, and I'll be outta here?"

—PENNY WIGGINS

Love for me has always been like a pretzel. Twisted and salty.

—EMMY GAY

My love life is like a fairy tale. Grimm.

—WENDY LIEBMAN

Love is one of the most powerful drugs there is. That's why they won't let you have it at work.

—SIMONE ALEXANDER

If love is the answer, could you please rephrase the question?

—LILY TOMLIN

You have heard the adage "You can't love another, until you can love yourself." I disagree. It may be difficult to enter into a healthy relationship whilst marinating in a quagmire of self-loathing. But it is a mere can of corn to devote twenty-three hours a day to obsessing over someone who is only vaguely aware that you borrowed the metro section of his newspaper at Starbucks.

—JANEANE GAROFALO

Love is like playing checkers. You have to know which man to move.

—MOMS MABLEY

Luck

I feel if I'm lucky, I'll fall in love. If I'm unlucky, I'll fall and hit my head.

—EMMY GAY

How lucky we are that we can reach our genitals instead of that spot on our back that itches.

—FLASH ROSENBERG

Lying

If a man lies to you, don't get mad, get even. I once dated a guy who waited three months into our relationship before he told me he was married. I said, "Hey, don't worry about it. I used to be a man."

—LIVIA SQUIRES

Dating is hard on guys. Guys just got really good at lying about how many women they have had, and now they have to lie about how many women they haven't had.

—DIANE FORD

Men like to lie. I met this guy on the Internet. He said he lives in a big house, hundreds of rooms, basketball court, and a big yard. I was ready to marry the dude, until I found out he was on death row. Men like to lie.

—LEAH EVA

m, n, o

Magazines

I got several subscriptions to women's magazines so I could get some beauty tips. But it turns out I only needed one magazine, because they've all got the same article every month: "30 Ways to Shape Up for Summer. No. 1. Eat Less, No. 2. Exercise More, No. 3. What was I talking about? I'm so hungry."

—MARIA BAMFORD

I read an article in one of those magazines the other day about the ten most popular places to meet a man. And the number-one place was the grocery store. I didn't know that. I've been running in on a Friday night for a box of Kotex and running out. Now I see what the problem is, some nice guy is probably looking at me, then looking at my basket thinking, "Well, she looks like a nice gal, but I'll catch her next week."

—MARIA MENOZZI

A lot of women write into magazines with these really petty complaints about men, like, "He spends too much time with his friends," or, "I think he might be cheating on me." Folks, I've been in some bad relationships before. Don't complain to me about men until you've been shot at.

—LIVIA SQUIRES

I know I need some kind of athletic activity in my life, so I subscribed to a couple of health magazines. There's nothing better than kicking back with a cigarette, a Budweiser, and *Prevention* magazine and reading about what nicotine, alcohol, and sloth will do to me. The anxiety alone raises my heart rate.

—CINDEE WEISS

My old boyfriend used to say, "I read *Playboy* for the articles." Right, and I go to shopping malls for the music.

—RITA RUDNER

I was reading something about Penthouse Pet of the Year the other day. That's a dubious title, isn't it? Pet of the Year. What do you have to do to get to that, go on the paper?

—ELAYNE BOOSLER

Men love looking at pictures of two naked women together in their *Penthouses,* but only if they're pretty. You get ol' Marge and Madge stepping out of a big rig after a long day in the seat, and guys are like, "Hey! That ain't natural."

—BRETT BUTLER

I don't understand the *Sports Illustrated Swimsuit Issue.* Bikini models in a magazine about sports? That'll make sense the day I see Dick Butkus in the Victoria's Secret catalog.

—SHEILA WENZ

Playboy never wants you to think the pictures are posed. "We just happened to catch Kathy typing nude on top of a Volvo this morning."

—ELAYNE BOOSLER

Why would anyone want to read *Soap Opera Digest*? You're reading gossip about people who don't exist!

—MARGOT BLACK

Women reading *Vogue* magazine about the latest fashions to come off the Paris runway is the same as you men looking at naked women in *Playboy*. We're both looking at places we're never going to visit.

—ANDI RHOADS

Making Out

Have you ever been drunk and making out with someone and you just feel like kissing, and he pulls his package out? I didn't ask for that. The way that I dealt with it was I just put my hand on it and left it there, very awkward. But I was remembering one time when I was a kid and my parents asked my brother to do the dishes and he just did them very badly, and they never asked him to do it again.

—MARTHA KELLY

Mammograms

Mammogram. You ever get one of those things? They put your breast in a vise and take it hostage. Start cranking it shut, like you have the secret rocket formula. You don't think it's ever going to get back into its natural shape again; you'll be rolling it up to get it back in the bra. Put a little ham key on the end of it.

—MARGARET SMITH

Manners

My man won't open my door or pull out my chair. But the minute
we're alone, he wants to open my legs and pull down my undies.

—LAURIE MCDERMOTT

Marathons

The only sport I absolutely refuse to watch: marathon running. It looks
like a bunch of anorexics in a hurry to get a burger. I can't watch it.
Do twenty-six miles, you're running from something, that's all I'm saying.
Sit down. Think about it.

—KATHLEEN MADIGAN

What would make seventeen thousand people want to run for twenty-
six miles? All I could figure out was maybe there was a Hare Krisnha in
back of them going, "Excuse me. Could I talk to you for just a second?"

—RITA RUDNER

Marriage

I'm not interested in marriage. But everyone always asks, "Don't you
want to meet that special guy?" Hey, I meet special guys all the time.
And if I was married, I'd have to stop doing that.

—LEE ARLETH

I don't want to get married because I don't like the idea of sharing
income with a guy. I mean, I don't make that much money as it is, and
I need all of it for gambling.

—COURTNEY CRONIN

Everyone in my family asks me, "When are you getting married?" Which means, "We know you're doing it, and we're tired of feeding you."

—MONIQUE MARVEZ

My take on marriage is this: Why buy the butcher when you can get the sausage for free?

—JEN KERWIN

My husband and I didn't sign a prenuptial agreement. We signed a mutual suicide pact.

—ROSEANNE BARR

Whenever anyone in our family announces that they're getting married, my first thought is, "How many months along is she?"

—WENDY WILKINS

I love being married. It's so great to find that one special person you want to annoy for the rest of your life.

—RITA RUDNER

My parents were worried about me getting married, so I got married. But they have a problem with it: She's black. But she's also a doctor, so it's okay.

—MARLA LUKOFSKY

When you first get married you run around and play games, "Catch me, catch me!" Now we play "Catch me," but we walk. "Can I catch you tomorrow?" Sure, I'll know in advance and have time to shave my legs.

—JOAN RIVERS

Marriage is very difficult. Marriage is like a five thousand–piece jigsaw puzzle, all sky.

—CATHY LADMAN

Most of the women in my family married for money, but not a lot of money. You can't go to a reading of a will in my family without someone asking, "Who's gettin' the tools?"

—LAURA KIGHTLINGER

My mother always said, "Don't marry for money. Divorce for money."

—WENDY LIEBMAN

I was too young when I got married—nineteen. They ought to lock up nineteen-year-old girls in closets until those hormones stop playing ping-pong with their brains. Because I was just walking stupidity looking for a place to land.

—DIANE FORD

Marriage is all about him. What he wants, what he needs. What about what I want, what I need? I need love, I need attention, I need a new BMW.

—LAURIE MCDERMOTT

The problem with marriage is that it involves men and women. And that's a pretty bad match.

—CATHY LADMAN

People say, "Listening is the key to a successful marriage." Ha. Whenever I listen to what my husband is saying, all I hear is, "It's true, I married an asshole."

—LAURIE MCDERMOTT

There's a study in Maine that found if you marry someone who doesn't appreciate you, tries to control you, and always has to be right, you may be unhappy. They also discovered that going without water for long periods of time makes you thirsty.

—CAROLINE RHEA

Never go to bed mad. Stay up and fight.

—PHYLLIS DILLER

Getting married is a lot like getting into a tub of hot water. After you get used to it, it ain't so hot.

—MINNIE PEARL

Monogamous sex isn't boring. It's like a really great book that you don't want to end—and then it doesn't.

—BETH LAPIDES

That's why I'm afraid of marriage. You have to make love to the same person for, like, three hundred years. How do you keep it exciting? Hats?

—ELAYNE BOOSLER

Sex when you're married is like going to the 7-Eleven—there's not much variety, but at three in the morning, it's always there.

—CAROL LEIFER

I'm married now, so I have to do my dating on the Internet.

—THYRA LEES-SMITH

I've been married awhile. You know you've become too dependent on your husband when you ask him to scratch an itch you can reach yourself.

—ROBERTA ROCKWELL

My husband and I are in what some call the "nesting" stage of marriage. Others refer to it as "The Running of the Visa" or "The Sex Is Getting Boring, Let's Buy Furniture."

—CHRISTINE BLACKBURN

My mom had good advice for me about how to stay married for a long time. She said, "Always remember, honesty is very important. It must be avoided. And the most important thing is, you have to let your husband be himself and you have to pretend he's someone else."

—RITA RUDNER

They say marriage is a contract. No, it's not. Contracts come with warranties. When something goes wrong, you can take it back to the manufacturer. If your husband starts acting up, you can't take him back to his mama's house. "I don't know; he just stopped working. He's just laying around making a funny noise."

—WANDA SYKES

Statistics show that the older you are when you get married, the more likely it is you'll stay together. Of course, because at eighty-five you can't hear how boring he is.

—CHRISTINE O'ROURKE

Till death do you part, that's biblical. But they didn't live long in those days, they had good plagues. Soon as that guy got on your nerves, here come some locusts to eat his ass. Now we got antibiotics, personal trainers, and tofu. We hang around forever. You end up just looking at each other, "I see you got up today. You should start smoking."

—WANDA SYKES

My parents have a very good marriage; they've been together forever. They've passed their gold and silver anniversaries. The next one is rust.

—RITA RUDNER

My parents have been married for fifty-five years. The secret to their longevity? "Outlasting your opponent."

—CATHY LADMAN

Know what I missed most at the end of my marriage? Putting my cold feet on the back of his warm legs at night. I used to love that. But then it stopped bothering him, so I quit doing it.

—DIANE FORD

I was married for two years. Which is a long time if you break it down into half-hour segments.

—CHARISSE SAVARIN

My mom is on her eighth husband. Federal legislation to keep gay people from getting hitched was called the "Defense of Marriage Act," but if they really want to defend marriage they'd pass a law that prohibits my mother from coming within one hundred yards of a Las Vegas wedding chapel.

—KELLI DUNHAM

Massages

I'm trying to get stress out of my life. I had a massage about a month ago. Have you had one? Did they put the whipped cream on you, too? It's a weird thing the first time getting a massage because you're lying on a table naked, being touched by a stranger. Which is very, very nice. They try and relax you. He played music, which was a little aggravating. The trombone kept hitting me in the head . . . at least I think it was a trombone.

—ELLEN DEGENERES

My husband likes massages. I booked a masseuse to come to the house. Wasn't that a good idea? I thought so, until the doorbell rang, and there was an eighteen-year-old blonde girl standing there, saying, "I'm here to give your husband a massage." I said, "He's dead."

—RITA RUDNER

Masturbation

I want to show you my breasts and yet I'm frightened. I don't know what it is, but I touch them. They're fabulous. I had no idea. I think I'll go home with myself. Bye, gotta run. It's so great to be coy with your own body. "Hey, wanna go out?" "Get lost, scum. Beat it." Try spending the night alone with yourself sometime. You wake up the next morning, nobody will ever know what you were doing, not even you. "You wore me out. It was insane. I loved it."

—SANDRA BERNHARD

Maturity

The older I get, the simpler the definition of maturity seems: It's the length of time between when I realize someone is a jackass and when I tell them that they're one.

—BRETT BUTLER

Medical Care

In the hospital, I didn't have the best care. An intern tried to get an IV into my arm fifteen times. Finally they had to get a junkie from the rehab ward to do it.

—HEIDI JOYCE

Medical Insurance

My HMO is terrible. They charge me for a self-breast examination. It's a flat fee.

—WENDY LIEBMAN

It takes so damn long to see a doctor, I think my HMO's trying to kill me. I called to get a strange mole checked out, but the first available appointment was in six months. I said, "By then, I could be dead." And the receptionist replied, "If that happens, be sure to cancel your appointment."

—STEPHANIE SCHIERN

My HMO only allows for thirty days of psychiatric coverage. That doesn't sound like enough. I've heard of the twenty-four-hour flu. I've never heard of the thirty-day crazy.

—LEIGHANN LORD

I'm looking into a new health insurance plan. I thought, I'm a woman; I should really ask if they cover abortions. Then I remembered, I never have sex and I'm not on the pill. So if I do get pregnant, I'd probably have the baby Jesus.

—JANINE DITULLIO

I lost my front tooth, and my insurance company wouldn't cover its replacement, claiming it was for "cosmetic purposes." So what's a root canal, an entertainment expense?

—STEPHANIE SCHIERN

I finally have a dental plan. I chew on the other side.

—JANINE DITULLIO

Medication

I've taken so much St.-John's-wort that I now have a wart, but I'm not depressed about it.

—LEMAIRE

In Mexico, prescription drugs are available without a prescription. As though self-diagnosis, that's the wave of the future. Which is ridiculous because there are a lot of freaks like me who'd be at the drugstore every day, going, "I have a brain tumor. What have you got for it behind the counter?"

—KATHLEEN MADIGAN

My male roommate and I mixed up our nicotine and testosterone patches. He got cranky and hungry. I got a raise and a corner office.

—KAREN RIPLEY

Meditation

I took up meditation. I like to have an espresso first just to make it more challenging.

—BETSY SALKIND

Memory

Men forget everything; women remember everything. That's why men need instant replays in sports. They've already forgotten what happened.

—RITA RUDNER

Men

I hate that book *Men Are from Mars, Women Are from Venus* because men aren't from Mars, men are from women. Men come out of women, so if they're screwed up, it's all our fault. Stop trying to blame it on other planets.

—CATHRYN MICHON

Men are simple things. They can survive a whole weekend with only three things: beer, boxer shorts, and batteries for the remote control.

—DIANA JORDAN

Men are like flowers. If you don't know how to handle a rose, you get stuck by a couple of pricks.

—MARGOT BLACK

I wish men would get more in touch with their feminine side, and become self-destructive.

—BETSY SALKIND

Men are like pay phones. Some of them take your money. Most of them don't work, and when you find one that does, someone else is on it.

—CATHERINE FRANCO

It seems to me that men ask a lot of questions, but they're not willing to do the research. They're always asking, "What do women want? What do women want?" Why don't they try buying us a bunch of stuff and see what happens?

—LIVIA SQUIRES

What do men want? Men want a mattress that cooks.

—JUDY TENUTA

My mom always said, "Men are like linoleum floors. You lay them right, and you can walk on them for thirty years."

—BRETT BUTLER

My perfect man is smart, funny, good-looking, a good dresser, sensitive, and he won't chase other women. So what I figured out is that my perfect man is gay.

—KAREN HABER

I like my men the way I like my subways: hot, packed, and unloading every three minutes.

—JUDY TENUTA

The only perfect man is Mr. Ed. He's hung like a horse and can hold a conversation.

—TRACI SKENE

A good man doesn't just happen. They have to be created by us women. A guy is a lump, like a doughnut. So first, you gotta get rid of all the stuff his mom did to him. And then you gotta get rid of all that macho stuff they pick up from beer commercials. And then there's my personal favorite, the male ego.

—ROSEANNE BARR

Women love men with problems. We look at a troubled man the way an architect looks at a dilapidated building: "How can I renovate you?"

—VANESSA HOLLINGSHEAD

Men. I learned you can't be choosy. You can't worry about how they look. Fat, small—a good person could be inside. So now I'm dating a stroke victim. He's a very nice man, and I think he loves me. I think that's what he's trying to say. Either that or I'm standing on his foot.

—ELLEN CLEGHORNE

I'm at a point where I want a man in my life, but not in my house. Just come in, attach the VCR, and get out.

—JOY BEHAR

Men do not like to admit to even momentary imperfection. My husband forgot the code to turn off the alarm. When the police came, he wouldn't admit he'd forgotten the code. He turned himself in.

—RITA RUDNER

I hear a lot of guys complaining that they suffer from Nice Guy Syndrome. "I can't get girls. I'm too nice." Maybe it's because we're so used to assholes, you confuse us. You scare us, we think it's a trick. "Ohmigod, he opened the door for me! What's next, sleeping with my best friend?"

—ROSIE TRAN

I'm so sick of men saying that women have all the power, because men are slaves to their penis. What you mean is that the 1 percent of women who look like *Playboy* centerfolds can get you to do anything, and the other 99 percent of us can't get a tire changed at rush hour. "Excuse me, sir! Oh, I guess he's gotta go home to log on at the Pamela Anderson Web site."

—ANN OELSCHLAGER

Men are delusional. Hugh Hefner lounges around in a bathrobe with three live-in girlfriends. You know guys are sitting at home watching the Playboy Channel and thinking, "That could be me. *I've* got a bathrobe."

—DENISE MUNRO ROBB

The quickest way to a man's heart is through his chest.

—ROSEANNE BARR

If you want your man to totally worship you like a love goddess, act like a Ferrari: Make a lot of noise, and only start when he puts all of his money into you.

—JUDY TENUTA

I like manly men. I like you to do man stuff. I ain't that type of woman to be like, "Ooh, he won't go to the mall with me." I don't need you at the mall, okay? I know my role. You make the money, *I* spend it.

—TESS

Men are always calling me a strong woman. I hate when I hear that because it only means one thing . . . I have to be on top all night long.

—JENNIFER FAIRBANKS

Ménage à trois

I was out dancing, and this couple hit on me. They wanted to swing! What can you say when you've been propositioned by a couple? I was thinking really fast and said, "As a matter of fact, I'm already seeing a couple. And they'd be livid if I cheated on them."

—KATHY GRIFFIN

The closest I ever came to a ménage à trois was once I dated a schizophrenic.

—RITA RUDNER

Boys always like the threesome fantasy, right? I can't do that, I'm a jealous woman. If I get a girlfriend, I'm not sharing her.

—SULLY DIAZ

I'm not an advocate of three-way sex. They're like that *Lucy* episode where Lucy and Ethel are trying to stuff all the chocolate into their mouths. I tried a five-way once, but I'm too needy. Afterwards I was like, "So are we all in a relationship now?"

—MARGARET CHO

Menopause

I went in to see my doctor to talk to him about this menopause thing, because I don't know if I really want to do it.

—JANE CONDON

Why do they call it menopause and not meno-stop? And what do men have to do with it anyway?

—KAREN RIPLEY

Call in the period police, I have pre-menopausal stress syndrome. This is the fear that I'll never stop getting my period.

—KATE CLINTON

I exercise, I diet, I meditate. I still want to rip someone's head off. The only good thing about menopause is that it helps me get in touch with my inner bitch. Do you know why the menopausal woman crossed the road? To kill the chicken.

—JANE CONDON

A new study found that menopausal women who smoke are more likely to have hot flashes, and women who smoke while having a hot flash are more likely to burst into flames.

—CAROLINE RHEA

My grandma Ludie told me, "The good news is, after menopause the hair on your legs gets really thin and you don't have to shave anymore. Which is great because it gives you time to work on your new mustache."

—KAREN HABER

Menstruation

When you become a woman, you go to your mother, looking for guidance, comfort, information. You know what I got? "Ah Monique, that's your aunt with the little red suitcase. She's going to visit once a month." I said, "You tell that bitch I moved and left no forwarding address."

—MONIQUE MARVEZ

I needed a pint of Ben and Jerry's Super Fudge Chunk and box of tampons. Pretty much if you're shopping for one, you're shopping for the other. The cashier checked me out and asked, "Paper or plastic?" I said, "Oh, I don't want a bag. I just want to walk down the street with these things out in front of me and watch people get out of my way."

—SABRINA MATTHEWS

I hate my period because it interrupts my life. Last month I couldn't have sex for a whole week. But it's better than the alternative: Kids interrupt every day of the month.

—JOHNNYE JONES GIBSON

I would like it if men had to partake in the same hormonal cycles to which we're subjected monthly. Maybe that's why men declare war, because they have a need to bleed on a regular basis.

—BRETT BUTLER

Sometimes straight men freak out when I talk about my period. But I guarantee that if straight men had a period, you would never hear the end of it. And you know they would never have protection. They would be using old socks and coffee filters: "Dude, let me get that sports section when you're done." Every bachelor apartment would look like a murder scene.

—MARGARET CHO

Mental Disorders

Six million people in this country are obsessive compulsive. Actually it's only five people. We just keep filling out the survey over and over again.

—SIMONE ALEXANDER

Military

Remember the whole controversy about whether or not women in the service should be in combat? Can women fight? Can women kill? Yeah, I think so. Just have the general come over and say, "Hey, see the enemy over there? I just heard them talking. They say you look fat in your uniform."

—ELAYNE BOOSLER

On gays in the military: Conservatives are worried straight men might become targets of sexual overtures. In other words, men in combat might have to face the same hell that's confronted secretaries and waitresses for generations.

—BEVERLY MICKINS

If we wanted to be part of an institution that is hostile to gays and women, we could just stay home with our families.

—GEORGIA RAGSDALE

Don't ask, don't tell. How dare they ask you to die for your country but ask you not to say who you are. As if you could win a war without lesbians. Who's gonna read the map?

—MARGARET CHO

Ban gays and lesbians in the military? Are you kidding? If you took all the lesbians out of the WACs, you'd be left with four typists.

—ROBIN TYLER

I spent five years in the Air Force, and if it wasn't for sexual harassment no one would have talked to me at all. An officer accused me of being a lesbian. I would have denied it, but I was lying naked on top of her at the time.

—LYNDA MONTGOMERY

The whole idea of the military strikes me as completely absurd. What sense does it make to go off somewhere thousands of miles away to a scorching desert, to kill a lot of people who have never done anything to me, when I can sit in the air-conditioned comfort of my own home and take out a few people who really matter?

—E. L. GREGGORY

Vietnam vets, I have a lot of empathy for them. They had to go to a horrible place and perform a hideous job for people who didn't even appreciate it. I know what that's like; I used to be a waitress at Denny's.

—ROSEANNE BARR

Mr. Right

Mr. Right is hard to find. This one chick said, "*I married Mr. Right!*" I'm like, "Hope you get a divorce soon, because I'm waiting for him." And a new job; she was my boss.

—JAYNE WARREN

I married Mr. Right. Mr. *Always* Right.

—LOTUS WEINSTOCK

Models

I'm not a model and that's okay with me. Because I don't want to look like a whippet or any other shaky dog.

—KAREN KILGARIFF

Models have such skinny bodies that their heads look big. The high-fashion look they're going for is Pez dispenser.

—LEMAIRE

I found this site where models are selling their eggs over the Internet. Oh, great, that's what this world needs, more vanity. Not more Einsteins or Picassos; more anorexic, catwalking hat racks.

—KRIS MCGAHA

I hate fashion. I hate that we reward people for being genetic freaks. They have these runway shows with a commentator saying, "A pretty face is your best asset this season." As opposed to last season, when ugly girls had a free ride.

—JANEANE GAROFALO

Money

My parents say, "A penny saved is a penny earned." If that's true, then my vacuum is the World Bank.

—LESLEY WAKE

The U.S. Treasury is trying to decide what to put on the backside of a quarter. There's overwhelming support for "Got laundry?"

—BONNIE CHEESEMAN

Excuse me, you middle-aged, Minoxidil millionaires, but why can't you figure out that the nude blonde who lives in your jockstrap is working her way up to your wallet?

—JUDY TENUTA

A girl who takes money for sex is a ho. Not me, I'm a gold digger. A ho is for rent, a gold digger is a thirty-year mortgage.

—ELAINE PELINO

Someday I want to be rich. Some people get so rich they lose all respect for humanity. That's how rich I want to be.

—RITA RUDNER

Monogamy

I meet guys who absolutely have no concept of monogamy. They think it's a game by Milton Bradley.

—CATHY LADMAN

Monogamy is really weird, like when you know their name and everything.

—MARGARET CHO

Monthlies

I've been sort of crabby lately. It's that time of the month again—the rent's due.

—MARGARET SMITH

Morning

How many women like to have sex in the morning? Now how many like to be awake when it happens?

—MARSHA WARFIELD

Motherhood

Before I became a mother I was such a free spirit. I used to say, "No man will ever dominate me." Now I have a six-year-old master.

—SULLY DIAZ

I'm a mom. I have two boys. Two teenage boys. Otherwise, everything is fine.

—JANE CONDON

You get a lot of tension, you get a lot of headaches. I do what it says on the aspirin bottle: Take two and keep away from children.

—ROSEANNE BARR

I have two kids, and over the years I've developed a really relaxed attitude about the whole child-rearing thing. I don't cry over spilt milk. Spilt vodka, that's another story.

—DARYL HOGUE

The way I feel, if the kids are still alive when my husband comes home from work, I've done my job.

—ROSEANNE BARR

I'll be a real good mother. I've been called one.

—WENDY LIEBMAN

I'd like to have kids. I get those maternal feelings. Like when I'm laying on the couch and I can't reach the remote control.

—KATHLEEN MADIGAN

I think I'd be a good mother, maybe a little overprotective. Like I'd never let the kid out—of my body.

—WENDY LIEBMAN

I don't think I'll ever have a mother's intuition. My sister left me alone in a restaurant with my ten-month-old nephew. I said, "What do I do if he cries?" She said, "Give him some vegetables." It turns out jalapeño is not his favorite.

—JANINE DITULLIO

As a mom, I'd hate to hear "Mom, who do you love most?" Because then I'd have to say, "You know, I never wanted children."

—LAURA KIGHTLINGER

Mothers

My mom breastfed me. It was only 2 percent.

—WENDY LIEBMAN

This was as mad as my mother ever got: "Y'all quit. Don't make me stop this car." "Mama, you're not in the car, you're in the hammock with a jelly jar full of Scotch." Then she'd say, "Wait till your father gets home." "Mama, it's been eight years."

—BRETT BUTLER

I got my sense of humor from my mother. When I was growing up, she refused to bake. She said, "Well, you just eat it."

—BETSY SALKIND

My mom used to always walk around the house talking stuff about, "I don't care what you do when you get your own place, but as long as you're living here . . ." Oh, I couldn't wait to move out, and get my own place, and invite my mama over.

—MELANIE CAMACHO

My mother wasn't the protective type. When my father left, she told us kids, "Don't think this just had to do with me. Your father left all of us."

—CAROLINE RHEA

My mom had a range of two emotions: She was either pissed or trying to get you to feel bad for her. As a kid, she told me how she learned to swim. She got in a boat and someone took her out in the middle of a lake and threw her into the water. I said, "Mom, they weren't trying to teach you to swim. When they shot at you, they weren't trying to teach you to deflect bullets."

—PAULA POUNDSTONE

My mom is one of those really angry moms who gets mad at absolutely everything. Once when I was a little kid, I accidentally knocked a Flintstones glass off the kitchen table. She said, "Well, dammit, we can't have nice things."

—PAULA POUNDSTONE

When I was nine years old this guy went on a date with my mother and me. He was a hardcore bachelor and thought I could be entertained for hours with a stuffed animal, locked away in the den while he made out with my mother in the living room. At this point I'm like, "Russell, I know what you want." Then all of a sudden we have this bargain going on like I'm my mother's pimp, "Russell, let me tell you something about the mommies in my stable. They're quality pieces, and I can't let you have this one for anything less than a Monopoly game and an Eagles album; make that a double album."

—LAURA KIGHTLINGER

My mom is always on the prowl trying to find potential suitors for me, but she's gone over the edge. My brother had a little fender bender, and my mom was trying to set me up with all the men at the scene of the accident. "What about the cop?" "No, Mom." "The tow truck guy?" "Mom!" "What about the guy who hit your brother?" "He was driving drunk!" "You're so quick to judge people."

—LORI GIARNELLA

My mom taught me everything I needed to know. Don't talk to strangers, don't pay retail, and the size of your hair should always match the size of your ass.

—STEPHANIE SCHIERN

My mother just wrote her autobiography. Pick it up. It's in the stores right now. It's entitled *I Came, I Saw, I Criticized.*

—JUDY GOLD

Saw my mom today. It was all right, she didn't see me.

—MARGARET SMITH

I like to talk to my mother every single day because hearing how delusional I may become one day makes me appreciate every day that I have left with my sanity.

—TAMI VERNEKOFF

When my mother makes out her income tax return every year, under "occupation," she writes in, "Eroding my daughter's self-esteem."

—ROBIN ROBERTS

I hope all my blood tests come back as negative as my mother is.

—KATE MASON

My mom is very possessive. She calls me up and says, "You weren't home last night. Is something going on?" I said, "Yeah, Mom. I'm cheating on you with another mother."

—HEIDI JOYCE

I just got back from visiting my family. This is how my mother greeted me. "Honey, you are not coming in the house in that baggy jacket. Why don't you give it to some fat person?" I said, "Here, take the jacket, Mom."

—JANINE DITULLIO

My mother is so passive-aggressive. She says things to me like, "You just can't seem to do anything right, and that's what I really love about you."

—LAURA SILVERMAN

There's an old saying, "Neurotics build castles in the air, and psychotics live in them." My mother cleans them.

—RITA RUDNER

I'm trying to keep my mother from calling me every day. I moved two thousand miles away, she calls me to tell me how high the phone bills are. My sister bought her a computer and taught her e-mail. So now my mother e-mails me and then calls me to tell me she sent me e-mail. If I respond, she calls me to tell me she got the response and then keeps me on the phone for a half hour about what she just e-mailed. Instead of one call a day, I'm now getting twenty-four calls and sixteen e-mails with the other eight or so calls being, "Did it go through?" Yes, about forty times. Stop pressing "send." I had to report my mother for spam.

—MARIA MENOZZI

My mom, she wakes me at six in the morning and says, "The early bird catches the worm." If I want a worm, Mom, I'll drink a bottle of tequila.

—PAM STONE

My mother and I had different attitudes toward sex. She said, "Whatever you do, never sleep with a man until he buys you a house." Well, it worked for her, and I got a swing set out of the deal.

—JUDY BROWN

My mother is sixty, and her whole life she only slept with one guy. She won't tell me who.

—WENDY LIEBMAN

My mother says, "If I get senile, just put me in a home. I don't want to be a burden to you." And I say, "Mom, I'd shoot you dead before I would do that."

—LAURA SILVERMAN

God bless my mom, she had reverse Alzheimer's. Towards the end she remembered everything, and she was pissed.

—S. RACHEL LOVEY

If you're looking for a way to piss your mother off, here's what I suggest. Next time you're driving with your mother, stop in front of the local strip joint. Put the car in park and say, "I'll be right back. I just have to run in and pick up my check."

—JUDY GOLD

Mourning

My Aunt Sylvie's husband died thirty years ago and she can't get over it. She turns everything he owned into something. "So what do you think of this necklace? It's Dave's belt buckle." Then she said, "What do you think of these ball earrings?" I'm like, "I don't even want to know."

—JUDY GOLD

Movies

I'll never understand why people go to movie theaters to have conversations. Going to the movies to talk is like going to a restaurant to cook. The idea is that you have paid your money to have someone do something better than you can do it yourself.

—RITA RUDNER

My boyfriend won't see anything he terms a "chick film." That's any film where the woman talks.

—MAURA LAKE

I saw the movie *Jackass* and the feminist in me was offended there weren't any women participating in the stupid stunts. But then I realized there are already women doing jackass stuff on videotape. It's called porn.

—WENDY WILKINS

I've always tried to be as cool as the Bond girls, but they don't remind me of any women I know. Sleeping with him one second, forgetting him the next. Where is the Bond girl who says, "James, I know we discovered the antidote to a rare tropical virus that threatened to destroy the earth, but why didn't you call? And who's that Korean kickboxer you're with? Did our trip in the submarine mean nothing?"

—MAURA LAKE

I really detest movies like *Indecent Proposal* and *Pretty Woman* because they send the message to women that sleeping with a rich man is the ultimate goal, and really, that's such a small part of it.

—LAURA KIGHTLINGER

Men never get too old for the entertainment industry. I saw a Clint Eastwood movie, he's around 110, and they have him in bed with a twenty-four-year-old. I demand some parity, a film where Tom Cruise sleeps with Phyllis Diller.

—MICHELE BALAN

I don't like movies, I like plays. This way, I can stand up and tell them it stinks.

—LINDA HERSKOVIC

Moving

We got a new house in Los Angeles and hired a vegetarian moving company. They were too weak to lift anything.

—RITA RUDNER

Music

I went to a blues bar last night, but the singer was in a good mood, so she canceled the show.

—DEBBIE KASPER

I used to want to be a country-western singer, but I took a test and I had too much self-esteem.

—BRETT BUTLER

I've written a country-western codependent song. It's called "If You Leave Me, Can I Come Too?"

—KATE CLINTON

Men who listen to classical music tend not to spit.

—RITA RUDNER

I love that Eminem song "I'm Sorry Momma, I'm Cleaning Out My Closet." Because now I could say to my teenager, "If Slim Shady can clean his damn room, so can you."

—CORY KAHANEY

That rapper 50 Cent. Everyone says, "50 Cent, he's tough. He's been shot nine times." Nine times! He doesn't sound tough to me, he sounds like a moron. Learn how to make friends, buddy.

—ROSIE TRAN

The song "If I Had a Hammer" is geared toward people who don't have a hammer. Maybe before I had a hammer I thought I'd hammer in the morning, and hammer in the evening. But once you get a hammer, you find you don't really hammer as much as you thought you would.

—ELLEN DEGENERES

They say violent music lyrics make men mistreat women. I think if a man is going to treat you bad, he's going to treat you bad. He doesn't need theme music.

—LEIGHANN LORD

Musicians

I used to be in a band. You may have heard of us, the marching band. I chose the tuba based on this theory: If you're not cool enough to be a cheerleader, make sure you're carrying something big enough to knock one on her ass.

—AMY BARNES

Mustaches

Guys are lucky because they get to grow mustaches. I wish I could. It's like having a little pet for your face.

—ANITA WISE

I love a man with a mustache. And fortunately for me, I've found a man who loves a woman with one.

—AURORA COTSBECK

Nails

I put on fake nails once, those surfboard Satan nails from hell. But I couldn't do anything; they're useless! The only thing they're good for is starting an orange. Or while you're choking . . . tracheotomy!

—SUE MURPHY

Looky look, I painted my nails orange to match the color of today's terrorist warning.

—CYNDI STILES

Naked

If God meant us to be naked he would have made our skin fit better.

—MAUREEN MURPHY

Names

Black people, you must stop naming your kids this crazy stuff. You're introduced to someone, and they walk away, and you're wondering, "Okay, one was Chandelier, and the other was Chlamydia?"

—RENÉ HICKS

My name is uBu, and I love it. It's an affirmation. I prefer it to my slave names: Wife, Mother, and my husband's favorite, Sexual Chocolate.

—UBU (IBME) ZURUB

My sister Susan Silverman got married to Joseph Abramowitz. They hyphenated their last names, so they're now the Silverman-Abramowitzes. But they're thinking of shortening it to Just Jews.

—SARAH SILVERMAN

Naps

Naps are wonderful, aren't they? Sometimes I have to take a nap to get ready for bed.

—MARSHA WARFIELD

No day is so bad it can't be fixed with a nap.

—CARRIE SNOW

Last time I baby-sat, when I told the kids it was time to take a nap, they got mad and started to cry. Can you remember when you didn't want to sleep? I guess that's the definition of adulthood: You want to sleep. If a three-year-old came up to me and said, "I'm beat, I have been working those Legos for an hour, the Big Wheel is jackknifed on the end of the driveway. I'm just gonna crash in the back room." I'd be like, "My, but you're mature. You go ahead. I'll hold your calls."

—PAULA POUNDSTONE

Neck Braces

I wore a neck brace for a year. I wasn't in an accident or nothin', I just got tired of holding my head up.

—MARGARET SMITH

Neighbors

I have this "I'm sorry" neighbor, who doesn't mean it but uses it to complain about something every night, "I'm sorry, could you turn your TV down? It's a little loud. I'm sorry, could you shut off all your appliances? Your electricity is very annoying. You're walking up there, too. Is that something you have to do? I'm sorry, but could you cut off your feet?"

—**LAURA KIGHTLINGER**

I like to watch TV with my neighbors because they have cable and a big-screen TV, and I've got binoculars.

—**SIMONE ALEXANDER**

Nephews

My two-year-old nephew is just learning to open and close a door, although he can barely reach the doorknob. Being his aunt, I'm going to teach him something practical, so we play Jehovah's Witness. I knock, he opens the door, and then slams it shut.

—**MARIA MENOZZI**

My nephews love spending time with me because I let them do anything they want; they're not my kids. Only thing I have to do is keep them alive, that's all. "Ice cream all day? Sure, I don't have to cook. Eat up, I don't pay your dental bills."

—**WANDA SYKES**

News

I was watching the news the other day, sponsored by Paxil. Now I need it, I watched the news. That's smart advertising.

—ELLEN DEGENERES

The annual report for an insurance company in Cleveland features the photograph of a naked eighty-two-year-old man. He said, "Wow! That's the last time I'm making a late payment."

—CAROLINE RHEA

Recently a sewer worker was rescued when he was trapped beneath the streets. I think the time to rescue him would've been when he first went to apply for the job.

—CYNDI STILES

Nipples

Here's something I've never understood: How come men have nipples? What's the point? They're like plastic fruit.

—CAROL LEIFER

Normalcy

Normal is just a cycle on the washing machine.

—WHOOPI GOLDBERG

Nostalgia

I was at a party where somebody was talking about "the good old days." I was like, "Which good old days? During the McCarthy blacklist? Or when blacks couldn't vote? When they burned women at the stake because they were herbalists? Those good old days?"

—BETH LAPIDES

Obscene Phone Calls

I received an obscene phone call in the middle of the afternoon. A guy called and said, "I'd like to bite you, give you a spanking, and ride you till you beg for more." I said, "Thanks for the offer, but I've already got a long-distance company."

—LAURA KIGHTLINGER

Obsessions

Irrational crushes, infatuations, or obsessions. Whatever you want to label it, it's important to reach out to others.

—JANEANE GAROFALO

Older Men

When I was seventeen years old, I was going out with a fifty-nine-year-old man. Sexually we got along great because the things he couldn't do anymore were the things I didn't know about.

—CAROL HENRY

I married an older man. Foreplay took a little longer, but at least his hand shook.

—JENNY JONES

The old saying was, "Marry an older man because they're mature." The saying now is, "Marry a young man, because men don't mature."

—RITA RUDNER

I'm back-dating my target group to older men. My girlfriends are always asking about my dates: "Is he cute?" I'm like, "I'll just settle for a healthy prostate."

—MAURA LAKE

Some people say older men have long endurance and can make love longer. Let's think about this: Who wants to fuck an old man for a long time?

—MARSHA WARFIELD

There ain't nothing an old man can do but bring me a message from a young one.

—MOMS MABLEY

Opportunity

Don't be afraid of missing opportunities. Behind every failure is an opportunity somebody wishes they had missed.

—LILY TOMLIN

Orgasms

In a lifetime the average person spends four hours out of 569,500 hours experiencing orgasm. And 62 percent of that is self-inflicted.

—LILY TOMLIN

Everyone has a different way to reach orgasm. For me everything has to be in harmony. My yin has got to be totally balanced with my checkbook.

—SIMONE ALEXANDER

I once had a girlfriend who was so guilt-ridden about being a lesbian that the only way she could have an orgasm was if we pretended to be shipwrecked, adrift at sea, far from civilization, never to return. So in order to make this whole thing realistic, I had to buy an inflatable raft, a foot pump, and a bailing bucket. Then I had another girlfriend who liked sex best under time pressure, when she had to rush. So we used to pretend that she was an air traffic controller who had ten seconds to come before two jumbo jets would collide in midair. That was exciting, the best nine and a half seconds of my life.

—SARA CYTRON

My boyfriend's always saying, "Livia, I can never tell if you've had an orgasm. I can never tell." I said, "Well, turn off the TV and get in here."

—LIVIA SQUIRES

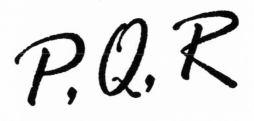

Pantyhose

My friends talked me into wearing a skirt for a job interview, but I don't wear pantyhose. I made a certain sacrifice, I bought foundation and covered up my tattoo, but the pantyhose just make my leg hair look real funny.

—SABRINA MATTHEWS

I hate pantyhose. Although I occasionally wear control top because I've found there's no quicker way to flatten my tummy and shut down my whole digestive tract.

—MERCEDES WENCE

I know a man invented pantyhose. When you're tall, they're a nightmare. People say, "Gee, you walk so demure." Not really. It's just that my crotch is down to my knees. So I decided to try the queen size. Well, that was handy. They doubled as a bra.

—KAREN RIPLEY

Parenthood

You don't know what love is until you become a parent. You don't know what love is until you fish a turd out of the bathtub for someone.

—MARGARET SMITH

Teenagers. They say they don't need you to be their friend. Yeah, no kidding. I know who my friends are, and they don't steal money out of my purse in the middle of the night.

—CORY KAHANEY

Parents

I was a mouthy child and when my mother had enough she'd say, "Come sit on my lap, and we'll look up orphanages."

—JACKIE KASHIAN

My parents were both in the Marine Corps. But I had a pretty normal upbringing: I stood guard duty at night just like all kids. And my mom made me wash the bathroom floor with a toothbrush, so I used hers.

—MARY GALLAGHER

My father's a proctologist. My mother is an abstract artist. That's how I view the world.

—SANDRA BERNHARD

My parents are real old-fashioned; they're not used to my lifestyle. I told my mother I spent the weekend at my boyfriend's house, and she got mad at me. She asked, "You know what they call girls like you?" And I said, "Yes, satisfied."

—MARIA MENOZZI

I got even with my parents. My parents came to stay with me for the weekend in my apartment. I made them sleep in separate bedrooms. My mother said, "What? Are you crazy? I've been sleeping with this man for years." I said, "Look, I don't care what you do on the outside. But when you're in my house . . ."

—ELAYNE BOOSLER

All my hippie friends are permissive parents. I think it's because what they name their kids makes discipline sound strange: "Sunshine Rainbow Girl, don't make me stop this car." "Daisy Flower Life and Sunset Rose, don't set fire to the dog!"

—KELLI DUNHAM

I took my parents back to the airport today. They leave tomorrow.

—MARGARET SMITH

My parents only had one argument in forty-five years. It lasted forty-three years.

—CATHY LADMAN

My parents are in their late sixties and they still have sex. Because they want grandchildren.

—WENDY LIEBMAN

Parking

I got a ticket for parking in a street cleaning space, which really pissed me off because there was no other space, and I'd left a note on the windshield that said, "No, no leave it, I'll get this area." Because I love to vacuum and I would have been happy to do that.

—PAULA POUNDSTONE

People aren't tense enough about the parking thing. Someone had to put up a smartass sign, "DON'T EVEN THINK ABOUT PARKING HERE." I tell you what. I stood there and thought about it. I did. I threw some pebbles up to get their attention. "Look. I'm thinking about it. Go ahead, call the cops and see if I care. I'll tell them I'm thinking about something else."

—PAULA POUNDSTONE

Patriotism

I'm from Finland, and I've been working for a long time trying to look, sound, and be as American as possible. I'm thinking of taking the easy way out: Get fat, stop voting, and invade a small country in the Middle East.

—LISA MANNERKOSKI

I've always tried to be a good American citizen. So I've made it a point to not learn any other language but English.

—BECKY PEDIGO

Penises

Men are so hung up on penis size. As if the sexiest thing a woman could say in bed is "ouch."

—MIMI GONZALEZ

I'm just a huge fan of the penis. Can I just say I love penises? They're just the greatest. And they're all different, like snowflakes.

—MARGARET CHO

Why do men name them? You hear them saying things like, "Well, Bobby's awake." You never hear women saying things like, "I'm sitting on Margaret."

—MARSHA WARFIELD

Perfume

I'm wearing a new perfume that I recommend. It's called Tester. And it smells different every time you use it.

—CAROL LEIFER

Why are women wearing perfume that smells like flowers when men don't like flowers? I've been wearing a great scent; it's called New Car Interior.

—RITA RUDNER

Personal Ads

Everyone is putting up personal ads now. It's not sleazy like it used to be. Listen to this one, "Professor emeritus instructor of anthropology looking for female kindred spirit to travel, seek, and explore. Must have enormous hooters."

—MONICA PIPER

A truly honest personal ad would say, "I want to date myself, only with more money."

—MAUREEN BROWNSEY

I'm a little embarrassed to admit this, but I've tried online dating. Well, I e-mailed a few seemingly normal guys, but I've never met any of them in person. Mostly because they stop writing before we can meet. So to save what little self-esteem I have left, I've turned it into a game. I see how quickly I can get a guy to stop e-mailing me. "Hi, Bob. I've really enjoyed our e-mail exchanges and I'd love to meet for coffee. Tuesday or Thursday would be best, because I really have to schedule my time, what with four kids from my three previous marriages."

—LORI GIARNELLA

It's hard to trust when dating through personal ads. To make the personals more truthful, I think there should be a Pinocchio effect. Whenever a guy lies, his nose would grow. No, better yet, his member would shrink. This would cut down on both the betrayal and the birth rate.

—CARYL FULLER

Stay away from the Internet personal ads. They give you a false sense of self. You start thinking you're a "playa" because you're juggling e-mails. I've spent so much time on them, when I turn on my computer I hear, "You've got problems. Turn me off and talk to a live person!"

—MIMI GONZALEZ

Pets

I've always had pets. I know I should have a child someday, but I wonder, could I love something that doesn't crap in a box?

—SHEILA WENZ

Pet cemeteries fill an important need for those who don't have trash cans.

—CYNDI STILES

Pheromones

One of my friends suggested that maybe my problems with men were based on pheromones. Great, that means I could be repelling men on a basic biological level. I'm like a citronella candle. Ladies, if you want a girls' night out and don't want to deal with aggressive guys, bad pickup lines, or free drinks—take me along. Put me in your group of friends, and I'll keep men away for up to six hours.

—LORI GIARNELLA

Philosophy

I got an A in philosophy because I proved that my professor didn't exist.

—JUDY TENUTA

Phobias

I suffer from peroxa-phemaphobia. Every time I've gotten near a beautiful blonde woman, something of mine has disappeared. Jobs, boyfriends. Once an angora sweater leaped right off my body.

—RITA RUDNER

Phone Sex

Phone sex on cell phones is so frustrating. Every time it starts getting good, the phone starts cutting out. I'm like, "Honey, I'm losing you. Can you feel me now? Can you feel me now?"

—DAVA KRAUSE

I have so much phone sex that if I had a child it would be born with a dial tone.

—PAULARA R. HAWKINS

If I have phone sex to avoid getting pregnant, is that caller IUD?

—MARGOT BLACK

What's embarrassing about phone sex is that the neighbors can hear me having sex, but they don't see anyone enter or leave my apartment.

—SUE KOLINSKY

There are twenty-five thousand sex phone lines for men in the U.S. but only three for women. Apparently, when we want somebody to talk dirty and nasty to us we just go to work.

—FELICIA MICHAELS

I'm not embarrassed about having called one of those phone-sex lines. I dialed 976-HERS, just for the gals. My ex-lover answered. It was just like old times: She came, we fought about the cats, and I paid for sex.

—KAREN RIPLEY

I used to do phone sex. You've seen those ads, young women in lingerie, squealing, "Hi! Call us." So like an idiot some guy calls. He gets me. I'm lounging in my Lane Bryant nightgown, which is kind of frayed from opening and closing the refrigerator so much. I've got a couple of cats on the bed. I've got a Big Gulp, I've got a big burrito.

—MARILYN

Photographs

I came across this picture in our family photo album, and I don't know what to make of it. My mom, pregnant, cigarette dangling, mowing the lawn, and my little sister in an overturned playpen with a rock on top of it. And then there's me, tied to a tree with a jump rope.

—JANEANE GAROFALO

My boyfriend broke up with me last year for about two months. So I tore up all the photos I had with him in the picture. We got back together, and now he wants people to take pictures of us all the time. That's fine, but I leave just a little bit of space between us now in the picture. Just in case something happens and I look really good in that one.

—MARY GALLAGHER

Physique

Everything about me is God-given. God gave me the money to get a boob job. Okay, so God gave the money to some guy to give to me to get a boob job.

—ELAINE PELINO

Feeling shitty about your physique is an important state of mind, for it leads one into a series of diverse, unfulfilling relationships. As opposed to just one monogamous journey into the banal.

—JANEANE GAROFALO

I have flabby thighs, but fortunately my stomach covers them.

—JOAN RIVERS

I don't have an hourglass figure. I have an hour and a half.

—WENDY LIEBMAN

I sacrificed my body to the goddess of motherhood. I used to have a waist. I'm still keeping the pants because they fit around my head now.

—STEPHANIE HODGE

I hate skinny women, because no matter how thin, they're still always on a diet. My friend Cynthia is five-nine and 102 pounds, has been on Phen-Fen, Metabolife, and lives on Slim-Fast. Used to be she'd ask, "Do I look fat in this?" Now she says, "Can you still see me? Am I still visible to the naked eye?"

—KELLY MAGUIRE

Men try forever to preserve their old football image. My husband is shaped like one.

—PHYLLIS DILLER

Piercing

I used to have an apartment in L. A. with roommates that had nose rings, and I couldn't concentrate on a word they were saying without staring at their nostrils. They could've told me the apartment just burned down and I'd say, "Uh, did that hurt going in? Can you pick your nose?"

—JUDY GOLD

I think men who have a pierced ear are better prepared for marriage. They've experienced pain and bought jewelry.

—RITA RUDNER

A friend of mine got her clitoral hood pierced. I think that's disgusting. I would never do that. I'd get a clip-on.

—SARAH SILVERMAN

Plastic Surgery

I just had my first foray into plastic surgery. Here's a little advice for plastic surgeons: Never guess why the patient is there, let them tell you. "Liposuction?" "No." "Chin-sucking?" "No." "Boob job?" "No, no, no—mole on my back!"

—CAROLINE RHEA

They can take the fat from your rear and use it to bang out the dents in your face. Now, that's what I call recycling. It gives whole new meaning to dancing cheek to cheek.

—ANITA WISE

To maintain our family resemblance, my entire extended family had their noses done by the same doctor.

—JANICE HEISS

I've never had plastic surgery. I still have my own real breasts. I know, because when I lay on my back they roll underneath my arms, and I look like a hammerhead shark.

—LEMAIRE

I'm proud to say I've been living in L. A. for four years and still have all my original body parts. My ex was addicted to plastic surgery. In the few years we were together he got hair transplants, an eye-lift, two nose jobs, cheek implants and liposuction. It was like dating Mr. Potato Head. By the time he was done, I felt like I was cheating on him.

—KRIS MCGAHA

I've had so much plastic surgery if I have one more face-lift it will be cesarian.

—PHYLLIS DILLER

I don't plan to grow old gracefully. I plan to have face-lifts until my ears meet.

—RITA RUDNER

I don't have anything against face-lifts, but I think it's time to stop when you look permanently frightened.

—SUSAN NORFLEET

I'm only thirty-three, but the plastic surgeon told me I needed a forehead-lift. This is what I'd look like with a forehead lift: "It's Monday? You're kidding! It was just Sunday yesterday. Wow!" I'd look like I'm on an eternal search for a surprise party.

—CAROLINE RHEA

I call them the lizard women. You know, the ones who have had so much cosmetic surgery, they're no longer biodegradable. They look like giant Komodo dragons with Chanel accessories.

—BRETT BUTLER

Michael Jackson said he's only had two plastic surgeries. Yeah, and I only had two cookies for breakfast.

—CAROLINE RHEA

PMS

I thought I had PMS, but my doctor said, "I've got good news and bad news. The good news is, you don't have PMS. The bad news is, you're a bitch."

—RHONDA BATES

Women complain about premenstrual syndrome, but I think of it as the only time of the month I can be myself.

—ROSEANNE BARR

Political Parties

The Republication Party should change their national emblem from an elephant to a prophylactic, because it stands for inflation, halts production, protects a bunch of pricks, and gives a false sense of security when one is being screwed.

—ROBIN TYLER

Pollution

I confess that when I first read that smog is particularly hazardous to children, senior citizens, and physically active people, for a brief moment, I thought, "I'm in the clear for at least ten more years."

—PAULA POUNDSTONE

Pornography

My neighbor is in porn and I used to look down on that stuff, but I realize I'm just jealous that nobody has ever offered me money to have sex. Sure, a Bud Light and a basket of curly fries, but not cash.

—MARIA BAMFORD

In those dirty movies women are always having threesomes and orgies. I'm so lazy in bed, I couldn't be bothered. I just want a spotter: "Here, hold my leg up."

—TRACEY MACDONALD

Men love to watch two women make love. I wonder, does this turn them on, or are they just trying to figure out how to do it right?

—JOY BEHAR

Women don't like porno, we like erotica. Rent us sexy films with love and romance, get a bottle of the good stuff—Boone's Farm Strawberry Hill—and there'll be nothing left to you but a rumor and a baseball cap.

—MONIQUE MARVEZ

One night we were watching some porno and I thought I'd joke around a little bit. I said, "Wow, I've never seen a penis that big before. He's huge! Are they supposed to be that big?" My man was like, "Don't pay that any mind. They just do that with lights and stuff." I said, "Shoot, then we need to get us some of those lights in here."

—WANDA SYKES

My husband says I don't understand pornography because I'm always fast-forwarding to the story.

—ALICIA BRANDT

There's always some documentary on TV with a porn star named Juice Box saying how great the sex industry is: "I just love sex, and working in an unregulated industry that provides no legal recourse should I be repeatedly victimized kinda makes me feel hot."

—MARIA BAMFORD

I don't like porn, because I'm self-centered and don't get anything that doesn't involve me directly. I can't even watch the Food Channel, because I'm like, "Where's my Baked Alaska?" If I were watching a porn movie I'd probably be like, "Where's my really ugly guy from New Jersey with a hairy back and a bizarrely large penis?"

—CATHRYN MICHON

Power

Men in power always seem to get involved in sex scandals, but women don't even have a word for "male bimbo." Except maybe "senator."

—ELAYNE BOOSLER

Pregnancy

I took a pregnancy test, but I failed. I didn't expect to pass it, though. I didn't even study. And I got hammered the night before.

—JESSICA DELFINO

My period was late, and I had nothing to worry about, but I worried anyway: "Maybe I *am* going to have the Lord's child."

—PENELOPE LOMBARD

Let's face facts: It's kind of a minor tip-off that in the reproductive process, all stud puppets contribute is their seed. Oh, thanks, Jack in the Beanstalk. But we fertile femmes are the ones who power-bloat for nine months and give birth to some screaming mass of cells that will one day shoot us for the Mazda.

—JUDY TENUTA

I know lots of women who have had children. But I'm not sure it's for me. "Feel the baby kicking, feel the baby kicking," says my friend who is deliriously happy about it. To me, life is tough enough without having someone kick you from the inside.

—RITA RUDNER

By far the most common craving of pregnant women is not to be pregnant.

—PHYLLIS DILLER

I don't need a baby growing inside me for nine months. For one thing, there's morning sickness. If I'm going to feel nauseous and achy when I wake up, I want to achieve that state the old-fashioned way: getting good and drunk the night before.

—ELLEN DEGENERES

When my best friend had her baby she gained eighty pounds. Oh, don't think I wasn't photographed next to her every day. I never looked thinner. She was in total denial; she asked, "Do you think there's any chance this baby could weigh up to eighty pounds?" "No," I said. "I'm your best friend and I'm going to have to go with forty-five tops. And I feel that's quite a chunky baby, really."

—CAROLINE RHEA

They say, "A woman is at her most beautiful when she's pregnant." Then how come you go into the Bears' locker room and never see a poster of some nude babe in her third trimester?

—JUDY TENUTA

Presidents

It doesn't surprise me that Washington, D.C., is such a sexist place; it's a town that lives in the shadow of the Washington Monument, the world's largest dick. And there's never going to be a woman president, until somebody digs a seven-hundred-foot tunnel honoring Eleanor Roosevelt.

—CATHRYN MICHON

The president has done pretty much everything I expected him to do. The economy is in the toilet, we're at war, and everything is on fire.

—WANDA SYKES

They say we will never have a woman president of the United States because our hormones change once a month and it makes us crazy. Yeah, right. If a woman was president, she'd be like this: "Are you nuts? You take hostages on a day when I'm retaining water? I can't believe I have to sit here and waste my time with a morally bankrupt terrorist like you when there's a sale on and the stores close at six!"

—ELAYNE BOOSLER

I want to be president so I can be surrounded by Secret Service men. Those are real men. A guy who would take a bullet for me? That's so hot. Right now I can't even get a guy to take the wet spot for me.

—JENÉE

Procrastination

My mother said, "You won't amount to anything because you procrastinate." I said, "Just wait."

—JUDY TENUTA

Pro-Life

All of you who want to block clinics and deny the rights of others, here's what I propose: the buddy system. Have it your way, all these kids need to born, so now you get a buddy for eighteen to twenty-one years, federally assigned to you.

—JANEANE GAROFALO

The pro-life people, I say they should get a life. Because if they had one, they'd leave everybody alone.

—SUE KOLINSKY

I'd like the names of all the antiabortion people so that when all those kids start having babies, we can take them to their house.

—WHOOPI GOLDBERG

Promiscuity

My sister is a slut. She has this little ritual. She does this every morning. She gets up. She checks the mail so she can find the address, calls a cab, and gets herself the hell home.

—BONNIE MCFARLANE

My sister was so promiscuous she broke her ankle in the glove compartment of a car.

—PHYLLIS DILLER

Sometimes promiscuity can lead to unusual wisdom. For example, I had a friend in college who was very promiscuous. She'd been with so many guys in so many backseats that she could spell the name of every college in New England backwards. And she'd tell people she went to Darvrah U.

—JENNIFER POST

Prostitution

You wanna hear my personal opinion on prostitution? If men knew how to do it, they wouldn't have to pay for it.

—ROSEANNE BARR

I'd like to open a whorehouse for women so we can get it the way we really want it. Like, we pay our money and guys pretend they like talking to us and they care about our lives, then they have to hold us real tight and say, "Ooh, you're so thin!" Even if they've never seen us before, they have to say, "Have you lost weight?" And then we have sex, and right before that fabulous moment, they have to shout, "I can't believe how great your shoes match your dress!"

—KAREN HABER

Psychics

A good psychic would pick up the phone before it rang. Of course it is possible there was no one on the other line. Once she said, "God bless you." I said, "I didn't sneeze." She looked deep into my eyes and said, "You will, eventually." And damn it if she wasn't right. Two days later I sneezed.

—ELLEN DEGENERES

My mother thinks she's psychic. My whole life, my sisters and I have gone along with it, but I don't know how much longer I can keep up the charade. This week it's my turn to have an accident.

—MARGARET SMITH

Well, as I was driving, the phone rang. This was weird in itself, because the psychic had predicted that I would get a phone call later in the day. As it turned out, it was my psychic calling.

—ELLEN DEGENERES

Racism

I think racism is a terrible thing. I think we should all learn to hate each other on an individual basis.

—CATHY LADMAN

I think we can agree racial prejudice is stupid. Because if you spend time with someone from another race and really get to know them, you can find other reasons to hate them.

—BERNADETTE LUCKETT

There's a rule in Scrabble that forbids spelling out racist words. Who is this for? After a tough day of cross burning, how many hard-core racists are kicking back with Scrabble? And keep in mind, we're dealing with a group who spell *clan* with a "K."

—LEIGHANN LORD

I get nervous when people say to me, "I just can't tell any of you Asians apart!" Why do you have to tell us apart? Are we going to be separated for some reason?

—MARGARET CHO

I was walking down the street and this man actually calls me a Chink! I was so mad: Chinks are Chinese; I'm Korean—I'm a gook. If you're going to be racist, at least get the terminology correct. Okay, Bubba?

—MARGARET CHO

Reality

Reality is the leading cause of stress amongst those in touch with it.

—LILY TOMLIN

Recycling

I have a friend who's so into recycling she'll only marry a man who's been married before.

—RITA RUDNER

On recycled paper: I'm afraid that the wrapper on my McDonald's hamburger might once have been toilet paper.

—BECKY DONOHUE

Redecorating

Have you heard of feng shui? Apparently, if I paint my front door red, wealth and success will come my way. And that's a good thing because I won't be getting my security deposit back.

—CHRISTINE BLACKBURN

Don't try to discuss paint shades with your husband if you want to redecorate. If you say, "For the walls, I'd like a light peach base, with dusty rose and lavender accents ..." he'll just look blank. But say, "Let's make the kitchen look like a big black eye!" and he'll haul ass to the paint store.

—C. LYNN MITCHELL

We're redecorating and I didn't know how high to hang pictures, so I went to an art gallery. The expert there said to hang them at eye level. I'm five-six and my husband is six-two, so we have two hooks depending on who is home.

—RITA RUDNER

Refrigerators

I've been dreading opening my refrigerator because something is starting to smell bad. It could be the two-week-old broccoli, the casserole I can't identify, or my ex-husband in the freezer.

—DARYL HOGUE

Relationships

At the beginning of a relationship wouldn't it save so much time if you could just ask the guy, "Hey, are you an asshole?" And the guy could say, "Yeah." Which would be okay with me, because I go out with assholes. Exclusively.

—KAREN HABER

Relationships don't last anymore. When I meet a guy, the first question I ask myself is, "Is this the man I want my children to spend their weekends with?"

—RITA RUDNER

Men and women just look at life completely different. Women are playing chess; we plan relationships ten moves ahead. Meanwhile, the guy is playing checkers, thinking just one move ahead, "Jump me!"

—MARGOT BLACK

Long-distance relationships are hard. Especially when you both only have cell phones. It's like I don't become a girlfriend until nine P.M.

—DAVA KRAUSE

I just moved in with my boyfriend after having a two-year long-distance relationship. It's nice to do things together for a change. It's nice to go to the movies, have dinner together. Frankly, it's nice to have sex without having MCI involved.

—SUE KOLINSKY

I think I'm having low self-esteem about my relationship. I just failed one of those quizzes. One of the questions was, "When is it okay to start walking around naked in front of your new boyfriend?" I answered, "When you want to end your relationship."

—CAROLINE RHEA

If you are married or living with someone, then there is one thing that gets said day and night that drives both of you absolutely crazy. But one or both of you always says it. It is "What?" The word, the phrase, the implication, the irritation. "What?" "You're deaf?" "You mumble." "What?" "I don't mumble, stupid." "I heard that." "*That* you heard."

—ELAYNE BOOSLER

I didn't have sex for a long time. I have a boyfriend now, and I still don't have sex, because we live together. Now that the milk is free, we've both become lactose-intolerant.

—MARGARET CHO

You always know when the relationship is over. Little things start grating on your nerves: "Would you please stop that? That breathing in and out, it's so repetitious!"

—ELLEN DEGENERES

I wish our lovers treated us like apartments. They'd have to give us thirty days' notice before they left us, and they'd have to leave us in the same condition they found us in.

—DENISE MUNRO ROBB

I can't seem to make a relationship work. I'd give up trying if it weren't for all the cool parting gifts. You know, the stuff a guy leaves at your place he's not getting back. That's how I got half my CD collection, and all my porn.

—JOANNA BRILEY

I'm not shooting for a successful relationship at this point. I am just looking for something that will prevent me from throwing myself in front of a bus. I'm keeping my expectations very, very low. Basically I'm looking for a mammal.

—JANEANE GAROFALO

I love to shop after a bad relationship. I buy a new outfit and it makes me feel better. It just does. Sometimes I see a really great outfit, I'll break up with someone on purpose.

—RITA RUDNER

I can't get a relationship to last longer than it takes to burn their CDs.

—MARGARET SMITH

Some women go from one relationship to the next. Not me. It takes me forever to find a guy worse than the one I was just with.

—LEMAIRE

I'm not in a relationship now, but I have a stalker. Which is kind of nice, because at least he calls. And I never have to make plans with him, because he's always there for me.

—PAMELA YAGER

Religion

All religions are the same: basically guilt, with different holidays. "I feel so guilty. Let's eat."

—CATHY LADMAN

I was raised an atheist. Every Sunday, we went nowhere. We prayed for nothing. And all our prayers were answered.

—HEIDI JOYCE

The story of Adam and Eve made no sense to me. Eve is responsible for the entire decline of humanity because she was tempted by an apple. Don't you think God overreacted just a tad? It's not like Eve ate God's last Oreo.

—MARGOT BLACK

The books of religion are beautiful works of fiction. These guys were great writers who wrote addendums to suit their fancies and made arbitrary rules: the important thing being that we keep the women in the backseat, that's the main gist of all religions.

—JANEANE GAROFALO

I don't mind born-agains being born again, but why do they always have to come back as themselves?

—ROBIN TYLER

I was raised strict Irish Catholic. My mother wanted me to be a nun when I grew up. Which confused me, because she also was always saying how she wanted grandchildren. I told her, "Mom, you don't want me to be a nun, you want me to be a priest."

—ALEX HOUSE

I thought about being a nun for a while and believed I'd make a gol-darned good nun. Then I had sex and thought, "Well, fuck *that*."

—DIANE FORD

I'm Catholic, and my mother said we were born to suffer. So I married an attorney.

—MAURA LAKE

I joined the church, because I love bingo.

—JEAN CARROLL

I went to this big church wedding, and I don't go to church too often, because I'm Jewish. So I didn't know there were rules for going up for the snacks in church. My friend says, "You can't go up there, you're not confirmed!" Hey, I RSVPed; they knew I was coming.

—RANDY KAPLAN

I go to church to be uplifted from all the things that are going on in the world, and nothing makes me madder than when someone acts holier than thou. Quoting Scriptures and acting like they know the Bible backward. I fix them when I ask, "Since you think I have to prove my Bible study to you: What's Jesus' mama's maiden name, huh?"

—TONY SLAUGHTER

Most unselfish religion: the Jehovah's Witness. They think only 144,000 people are going to heaven. If you believed that, would you go door-to-door trying to get new converts? I'd be keeping that as a big secret. "I hear there are only eight seats left; shut up!"

—KATHLEEN MADIGAN

The world has been going haywire. Sex in the Catholic Church? Tsk, tsk, tsk. Stuff like that would never happen at Kingdom Hall. Know why? Too many Witnesses.

—NIKKI CARR

In pictures of Jesus he's always a blond, blue-eyed surfer dude. I don't know why. Jesus was Semitic, so he would have had dark eyes and hair, and a five-o'clock shadow. Basically, Jesus would look like a guy who'd make you nervous if he sat next to you on an airplane.

—JENNIFER POST

I'm Jewish but was raised not knowing anything about my religion. The only time we went to temple was to play bingo, so I thought Hebrew was pronounced "B-Four, O-Seventy Six."

—MICHELE BALAN

We were Pentecostal. When I was growing up we couldn't go to movies, we couldn't listen to rock music, couldn't wear makeup. That's just a lightbulb and a car away from being Amish.

—RENÉ HICKS

I love Judaism. It's the Classic Coke of religions.

—JANET ROSEN

There's only one difference between Catholics and Jews. Jews are born with guilt, and Catholics have to go to school to learn it.

—ELAYNE BOOSLER

Mormons are very organized. I had this neighbor, Mrs. Mabey, who stocked canned goods in her basement so she could be prepared for when Christ returns to Earth. Because apparently what Christ is looking for is creamed corn.

—NATASHA AHANIN

Moses was lost in the desert for forty years. You just know his wife was bitching at him. "I have asked you to stop and get directions for twenty-seven years. No, I'm not getting back on the damn camel, you're going to talk to someone, even if it's only that burning bush."

—KATHLEEN MADIGAN

The pope is a hard guy to please, isn't he? No weird sex. Well, what's this "kiss my ring" stuff?

—ELAYNE BOOSLER

Why is it when we talk to God we're said to be praying, but when God talks to us we're schizophrenic?

—LILY TOMLIN

I believe in reincarnation. I've had other lives. I know. I have clues. First of all, I'm exhausted.

—CAROL SISKIND

My husband thought reincarnation means you come back as a carnation.

—PHYLLIS DILLER

My mother's very religious. She's also very pro-war, because that's what Jesus would be. Smoke 'em out of their holes like a gentle carpenter.

—MARIA BAMFORD

The religious right is really getting out of control. Today they were at the grocery store blocking the home pregnancy test aisle.

—MELISSA MAROFF

When I taught Sunday school I was really strict. I used to tell the kids, "If one more of you talks, you're all going to hell!"

—MARGARET CHO

I had no idea there were so many private religious schools: the New Day Day School, the All God's Children Got Wings School, the All Homosexuals Must Die Middle School, the Apocalypse Pretty Soon School.

—KATE CLINTON

Every time I see a TV evangelist I can't help but think that if God wanted to talk to me through the TV, I think he could get a spot on a major network.

—MARGOT BLACK

Wouldn't it be great if we found you could only get AIDS from giving money to TV preachers?

—ELAYNE BOOSLER

If I had been the Virgin Mary, I would have said, "No."

—MARGARET SMITH

"The wages of sin are death." I would imagine so, but by the time they take the taxes out, it's just kind of a tired feeling, really.

—PAULA POUNDSTONE

Remarriage

I just got married. It's my husband's second marriage. If you think it's hard to get a guy who's never been married to commit, try to get a guy to go back and do it all over again. It's like talking a vet back into Vietam.

—CORY KAHANEY

Remarrying a husband you've divorced is like having your appendix put back in.

—PHYLLIS DILLER

I'm on my second marriage. You know when you let one guy get away, you're gonna have to build a taller fence and put better food out.

—BRETT BUTLER

I've been married twice. Both my husbands are remarried, very happy, and love each other very much. Somebody shoot me.

—SHEILA KAY

I'd like to get married again, but I'm afraid of that marital commitment—we're talking two, three years of my life.

—MAURA LAKE

I'm going to marry again because I'm more mature now, and I need some kitchen stuff.

—WENDY LIEBMAN

Remodeling

We just bought a house. My husband calls it a "fixer-upper." I call it a piece of crap.

—MARYELLEN HOOPER

We did some remodeling, and the workmen could have an attitude. The painter came, and I asked, "Could you fill in some of these holes before you start, please?" He said, "Lady, I don't spackle, I don't sand. I just paint." Then the exterminator came in. I said, "Kill the painter."

—RITA RUDNER

Respect

I met a guy the other night; I went home with him. I was going to have sex with him that night, but at the last minute I thought better of it. But I wound up staying over anyway. I changed my mind and had sex with him in the morning, which was nice and all, but then I spent the whole day wondering if he would respect me in the evening.

—LYNN HARRIS

Instead of asking a guy if he'll respect you in the morning, you should ask, "Do you have a job in the morning?"

—BONNIE CHEESEMAN

Restaurants

When going to a restaurant, "party of one" is rarely cause for celebration.

—ELLEN DEGENERES

At restaurants I don't mind if I order fish and it comes with the head on. I do mind it when I order beef.

—CYNDI STILES

My husband has never picked up a check in his life. People think he has an impediment in his reach.

—PHYLLIS DILLER

Eating out is very expensive. I was in one restaurant; they didn't even have prices on the menu. Just pictures of faces with different expressions of horror.

—RITA RUDNER

Why does Sea World have a seafood restaurant? I'm halfway through my fish burger and I realize, "Oh, my God, I could be eating a slow learner."

—LYNDA MONTGOMERY

If I ever got money, I would open a restaurant for single people. And I'd make 'em feel comfortable, too. Name it Just One. You walk in, nice long row of sinks. No tables and chairs. Everyone eats standing over the sink. All the food comes in the package, so you can read the back while you're eating.

—ELAYNE BOOSLER

I can't leave a restaurant without leftovers. Some restaurants actually get uncomfortable wrapping something up in tin foil, so they disguise it as a swan figurine. I'm like, "You might want to make that swan some babies, because I'm taking these Sweet 'N Low, too."

—MARGARET SMITH

Reunions

I went to the thirtieth reunion of my preschool. I didn't want to go, because I've put on like a hundred pounds.

—WENDY LIEBMAN

The good thing about going to your twenty-five-year high school reunion is that you get to see all your old classmates. The bad thing is that they get to see you.

—ANITA MILNER

Roadkill

How much roadkill do you think is actually suicide? Come on, some of those bastards are stepping out on purpose.

—KATHLEEN KANZ

Role-play

My husband and I were role-playing the other night and I started to cry when I realized that he'd cleaned the apartment.

—ALEX HOUSE

Romance

My mother always said that a rose is the perfect symbol of romance. It dies after a few days, its pretty petals fall off, and all you're left with is the ugly prickly thing.

—MAUREEN MURPHY

Running

My best friend subscribes to a magazine for runners. It seems like one issue could cover everything. But every month she keeps reading it and sending money for the next issue, and finally, they contacted her. They were like, "Look, we don't know what else to tell you. I guess, just keep running."

—TIG

P. Q. R

I don't run. I don't jog. I don't even like to walk fast. I mosey.

—DAVA KRAUSE

I bought Rollerblades to get in shape, because I don't want to run just for the sake of running. I'll run if I'm playing a game, or if I steal something.

—SABRINA MATTHEWS

The first time I see a jogger smiling, I'll consider it.

—JOAN RIVERS

I jogged for three miles once. It was the worst three hours of my life.

—RITA RUDNER

Sadomasochism

I've been thinking about S&M lately. Because if the guy ties you up, at least you know he wants you there for a while. It's a commitment.

—JANET ROSEN

Those S&M people, they are bossy.

—MARGARET CHO

I wonder, is pain always sexual for S&M people? If they're walking down the street, and they stub their toe, do they go, "Ow! I'm so horny"?

—SUZANNE WESTENHOEFER

Safe Sex

Everybody should practice safe sex. Because nobody wants to be doing it and put an eye out.

—EMMY GAY

The only way to really have safe sex is to abstain. From drinking.

—WENDY LIEBMAN

Safe sex is very important. That's why I'm never doing it on plywood scaffolding again.

—JENNY JONES

I'm scared of sex now. You have to be. You can get something terminal, like a kid.

—WENDY LIEBMAN

It's a little bit dangerous out there, and I guess men have to choose between marriage and death. I guess they figure that with marriage at least they get meals. But then they get married and find out we don't cook anymore.

—RITA RUDNER

Safety

I don't recall any overt safety features on anything when I was a kid, do you? Nobody put a bicycle safety helmet on my head. Holy cow, my dad could hardly wait to take off the training wheels before he shoved me down the hill.

—ELVIRA KURT

Safety was not a big thing when I was growing up. A seat belt was something that got in the way: "Ma, the seat belt is digging into my back." "Stuff it down into the seat. And roll those windows up, you're letting my cigarette smoke out."

—MARGARET SMITH

My nephew came over the other day, and he was wearing a helmet, shoulder pads, knee pads, gloves, and saying, "I'm a-gonna ride my bike." Where? Through a minefield?

—WANDA SYKES

I have six locks on my door, all in a row, and when I go out I only lock every other lock. Because I figure no matter how long somebody stands there, picks the locks, they're always locking three.

—ELAYNE BOOSLER

We had mice in our basement so I went to get some poison, but the tamper-resistant seal had been broken. I didn't know if I should buy it; someone might have slipped some aspirin in there.

—RITA RUDNER

Sales Work

My mother holds all the sales records for Avon ladies. Her secret was to follow Jehovah's Witnesses around so that people would be happy to see her.

—LYNDA MONTGOMERY

Scheduling

Everyone is always trying to cram so much into their schedules. I say fight back, take a stand, take a nap!

—MARGOT BLACK

School

Nothing I learned in school prepared me for life on any level. My first book should have read, "See Dick balance his checkbook. See Jane leave an unhealthy relationship. Run Jane run!"

—KATE MASON

I just found out that my oldest daughter is academically number one in her class. And she was nominated for prom queen. Thank you, it's not that big a deal, she's homeschooled.

—VICKI BARBOLAK

My parents home-schooled me when I was in the second grade. But the one thing I don't think they took into consideration was that they both worked all day.

—MARY GALLAGHER

I hate studying math, because there are all these rules. My mother says, "You make things too complicated." But I don't think so, because guys say I'm easy.

—HIJIRI SAKAKIBARA

I'm not good at math, I've never been good at math. I accepted it from a very early age. My teacher would hand me a math test. I'd just write on it, "I'm going to marry someone who can do this."

—RITA RUDNER

I was the total C student. If my son hands me his math homework, I'll have to say, "Hon, why don't you cheat off your little friends, or look it up in the back of the book like your father and I did."

—JANEANE GAROFALO

In high school, I could not pass a math test. I couldn't pass a drug test either. There may be a correlation.

—LYNDA MONTGOMERY

I had a typical high school romance. I was a cheerleader, and he was on the faculty.

—WENDY LIEBMAN

Science

Is there really such a thing as a black hole? I think someone just forgot to take the lens cap off.

—SIMONE ALEXANDER

Did you hear about those pigeons that found they could make lab technicians do anything they want just by refusing corn pellets?

—LILY TOMLIN

Scientists have been able to determine that cow flatulence is depleting the ozone layer. I'm embarrassed to say I've been walking around for years telling everyone it was the pigs' fault.

—NANCY WAITE

These two guys are now trying to clone human genes into cows so that you'd get cows that would give human milk. Or maybe you'd get girls with four really big tits. I'm sure they think, "Either way, big improvement."

—CATHRYN MICHON

If they can put a man on the moon why can't they put one in me?

—FLASH ROSENBERG

Science Fiction

I'm a big *Star Trek* fan, but do you remember the old one where there's a planet run by women, and they're all wearing miniskirts and white vinyl go-go boots? Right. Because if women were in charge of the planet that's what we'd decide to wear.

—SUE MURPHY

Self-acceptance

I honor my personality flaws. Without them, I'd have no personality at all.

—MARGOT BLACK

Don't compare yourself with someone else's version of happy or thin. Accepting yourself burns the most calories.

—CAROLINE RHEA

Self-analysis

I won't get into this whole self-analysis thing, I just won't. And I don't have to, because my boyfriend will do it for me.

—LAURA KIGHTLINGER

Self-destructive

I'm not a very self-destructive person, but mostly because I'm too lazy. I prefer to be in a relationship and let someone else do the work.

—MARGOT BLACK

Self-employment

I'm thinking about becoming my own boss. I have a pretty good chance of getting the job, because I'm already sleeping with me.

—JOY GOHRING

I work for myself, which is fun. Except for when I call in sick, I know I'm lying.

—RITA RUDNER

Self-esteem

I find low self-esteem incomprehensible. Why hate yourself, when you can hate others?

—AMY ASHTON

This guy dumped me because he said I have a low self-esteem. I said, "No kidding, I slept with you, didn't I?"

—TRACEY MACDONALD

I had a terrible childhood and my self-esteem isn't so great, so I haven't always picked the best men. But I have learned a lesson: If a guy tells you that he's a jerk, you should probably listen.

—SUE COSTELLO

Self-image

I'm getting very comfortable with my body. I'm sleeping on a full-length mirror.

—SANDRA BERNHARD

Self-involvement

He was the most self-involved guy I ever met in my life. He had a coffee mug on his table that said, "I'm the greatest." He had a plaque on the wall that said, "I'm number one." And on his bedspread it said, "The best." In the middle of making love he said, "Move over, you're getting in my way."

—KAREN HABER

Sensitivity

Men are sensitive in strange ways. If a man has built a fire and the last log does not burn, he will take it personally.

—RITA RUDNER

Separatism

When women go off by themselves, they call it "separatism." When men go off by themselves they call it "Congress."

—KATE CLINTON

Sex

Men keep rushing through lovemaking. Which is the part I like, the beginning part. Most women are like that. We need time to warm up. Why is this hard for you guys to understand? You are the first people to tell us not to gun a cold engine. You want us to go from zero to sixty in a minute. We're not built like that. We stall.

—ANITA WISE

Dr. Ruth says women should tell our lovers how to make love to us. My boyfriend goes nuts if I tell him how to drive.

—PAM STONE

I'm afraid to give instructions in bed because I'm afraid I'll get carried away. "Okay, pull my hair, and touch me right there. No, to the left. Now go outside and move my car so I won't get a ticket. Yeah, that's it."

—LAURA KIGHTLINGER

Making love to a woman is like buying real estate: location, location, location.

—CAROL LEIFER

For guys sex is like going to a restaurant. No matter what they order off that menu, they walk out saying, "Damn, that was good!" For women it don't work like that. We go to the restaurant, sometimes it's good, sometimes we got to send it back. You have those hit and misses, you might want to skip a few meals. Or you might go, "I think I'm going to cook for myself today."

—WANDA SYKES

Men reach their sexual peak at eighteen. Women reach their sexual peak at thirty-five. Do you get the feeling God is into practical jokes? We're reaching our sexual peak right around the same time they're discovering they have a favorite chair.

—RITA RUDNER

I overheard these two young guys talking about women and sex. One guy says, "It's so much easier for women to have an orgasm on top." And the other guy argued, "No, it's easier for women to have an orgasm when she's on the bottom." Finally, I turned to them and said, "Guys, actually it's much easier when we're alone."

—CORY KAHANEY

Cosmopolitan magazine says that a man reaches his sexual peak at eighteen, but a woman doesn't reach hers until thirty-five. Of course, we're not talking age, we're talking minutes.

—TRACI SKENE

My sex life is sometimes like Murphy's Law; if something can go wrong it will. Like one time during sex, my IUD started picking up radio stations. And what's worse is my boyfriend said, "Don't move. That's a really good song." All I can say is, if you've never seen a naked man play air guitar, count your blessings.

—MARIA MENOZZI

Men perform oral sex like they drive. When they get lost they refuse to ask for directions.

—CATHERINE FRANCO

My favorite sexual position is rich man on top, me on the bottom, looking up at my new five-carat diamond ring saying, "Yes, yes, yes, you're so big!"

—ELAINE PELINO

Guys always ask me how many men I've been with. Like I remember.

—CHANTEL RAE

Erogenous zones are so great. They can be anywhere on your body, and are different places for everybody. But probably for me, I swear to God, my biggest erogenous zone is my vagina.

—SARAH SILVERMAN

I said to my husband, "Why don't you call out my name when we're making love?" He said, "I don't want to wake you up."

—JOAN RIVERS

Every time we make love, my boyfriend keeps telling me to let him know when I'm having an orgasm. Which is difficult, because when I'm having one, he's usually not there.

—MARGO BLACK

How can you have sex without emotional attachment? Use an attachment.

—CARRIE SNOW

You know your sex life has dwindled when you get muscle soreness the next day after making love, like you just decided to take up running.

—LAURA HAYDEN

I want to be a tease, but I always go through with it.

—CHANTEL RAE

My last boyfriend liked to talk a lot during sex. He said it was because it turned him on, but I think he had ulterior motives because he always said the same thing, "Wake up, wake up, wake up!"

—CHRISTINE O'ROURKE

It's so long since I've had sex, I've forgotten who ties up whom.

—JOAN RIVERS

A terrible thing happened again last night: nothing.

—PHYLLIS DILLER

I read books that say if you want to keep sex hot, you tell the person what you want. How do you tell them you want somebody else?

—ELAYNE BOOSLER

Sex Education

People want to take sex education out of the schools. They believe sex education causes promiscuity. Hey, I took algebra. I never do math.

—ELAYNE BOOSLER

I grew up in a strict Catholic home, and I didn't have sex ed until I got to college. Man, I didn't know it was that easy to get an A.

—LEAH EVA

Sexual Aids

If you think your sex life might need a little spicing up, and you should find yourself, say, in a sex shop, let me give you some advice: Don't buy the chocolate body frosting. It takes sixty licks per square centimeter to get it off, and that stuff is filling. Basically, you're not going to get much out of it, unless you're the kind of person who only feels sexy after a big Thanksgiving dinner.

—LISA SCHROEER

Shampoo

If you want to attract a man, forget the strawberry and kiwi–scented shampoo. Get yourself some steak-scented shampoo and they'll follow you in droves.

—KELLY SMITH

Sharing

I have a problem with sharing, probably because I had so many brothers and sisters. When I was seventeen I got a marriage proposal but turned it down. Not because I was too young but because I'd finally gotten my own room.

—ROBERTA ROCKWELL

Shaving

Once I forgot to shave my legs for so long that when I went swimming, I caught fish. I think it's time for a shave when there's a widemouthed bass hooked to your thigh.

—SHEILA KAY

Shoes

High heels should be outlawed. At the very least there should be a five-day waiting period before you can buy them. They destroy your feet. It should be mandatory that the surgeon general print a warning label on high heels like they do on cigarettes. "Warning: These shoes can lead to lower back pain, aching toes, and the illusion that you are taller than you actually are."

—ELLEN DEGENERES

I hate it when you got to someone's house and they make you take your shoes off before you enter. What if the shoes make the outfit? I always wear a basic skirt and a sassy boot, so I can't be friends with those people.

—WENDY SPERO

I think high heels are ridiculous. It's like putting a building on the head of a pin.

—CATHY LADMAN

You can buy a four hundred–dollar pair of running shoes. And who sponsors marathons? Running shoes. And who wins every year? Some guy from Kenya who's never even had a pair of shoes.

—KATHLEEN MADIGAN

Niketown has display racks full of shoes specifically for hiking, climbing, golf, basketball, running, volleyball, skateboarding, soccer, and wrestling. I didn't buy anything because they didn't have a pair specifically designed for my sport, which is sitting.

—PAULA POUNDSTONE

I go into the store and the woman's like, "Hi, I'm Suzie. Welcome to Shoe Casa, where your shoe problems are my shoe problems. What's your size?" "I'm a size 10 wide." She's like "*Holy crap!* Code blue, code blue! Sasquatch, aisle four!"

—ERIN FOLEY

I had to go shopping at the tall-girls shoe shop. There was a basketball court in the basement in case anyone wanted to shoot hoops.

—JUDY GOLD

Shopping

Impulse buying is a bad habit. Like the time I bought a box of Pampers. Our son Billy was six years old and had been housebroken for over one year. When my husband questioned the purchase I said I was pregnant. Luckily, it slipped his mind and the subject never came up again.

—LILY TOMLIN

I'm a compulsive shopper. It's terrible, I buy things I don't need. Today I bought a jockstrap. I use it in my kitchen to hang garlic.

—CATHY LADMAN

I'm a shopaholic. I especially like to shop for shoes, because I don't have to take off the rest of my clothes. But if I do, I get a much bigger discount.

—BEA CARROLL

Buying something on sale is a very special feeling. The less I pay for something the more it is worth to me. I have a dress I paid so little for that I am afraid to wear it. I could spill something on it, and then how would I replace it?

—RITA RUDNER

I was shopping for groceries when I saw the sign for "feminine needs," and I thought to myself, "Finally, a store that sells nice, cute, well-hung guys with money who call when they say they're gonna. Where, oh where, are my double coupons?"

—LEAH KRINSKY ATKINS

I went shopping last week looking for feminine protection. I looked at all the products and decided on a .38 revolver.

—KAREN RIPLEY

I had a little accident with one of those girls who spray you with cologne in the department store. I had a book of matches and I hate to tell you what happened.

—BRETT BUTLER

I'm not a great shopper. I would rather shave my legs when I have goose bumps than go shopping.

—KATE CLINTON

Wal-Mart, the store for the openly cheap.

—CYNDI STILES

Men sure say the darnedest things. I went to buy a pair of eyeglass frames, and I couldn't make up my mind. So, 250 frames later, I finally find a pair I like. I turn to the salesman and ask, "How do you like these?" Big mistake. He says, "I think they make you look too brainy." "Oh," I said, "I didn't know women weren't supposed to look smart. Take these back and find me a pair that will make my boobs appear bigger, because with my prescription mine will be hugely magnified. Of course, I'll have to wear a disclaimer, 'Objects in glasses are smaller than they appear.'" Thanks, dude.

—MARIA MENOZZI

Ever go to the grocery store when you're at the end of a long line, the guy checking out creates sort of a snag in the operation, and the cashier has to call for backup? Well, we all hate that guy, but you know who I hate worse than that guy? The woman inevitably in front of me who feels compelled to turn around and say, "This is *ri-dic-u-lous!* Can you *be*-lieve this?" Ma'am, don't try to rally with me. *I hate you, too.* Maybe, after you successfully complete your transaction, you can turn around and we can talk, but until that time comes, please remain facing forward.

—SUSIE BARKER

Have you ever noticed the mannequins in the store have the natural look, the bra-less look. They have a sweater on with little points. Why would I buy a sweater that can't keep a mannequin warm?

—ELAYNE BOOSLER

I went into this one dress shop that was so exclusive, I didn't know you had to call ahead. The saleswoman asked, "Do you have an appointment?" I said, "No. Do the dresses have something else to do today?"

—RITA RUDNER

My new dress. It's from my favorite designer, On Sale.

—RITA RUDNER

I would rather have a sharp stick in my eye than go shopping.

—KATE CLINTON

Most men hate to shop. That's why the men's department is usually on the first floor of a department store, two inches from the door.

—RITA RUDNER

My husband takes me to Home Depot, I want to go home. "It's an entire aisle of nails! Get a sharp one, let's go!"

—MARYELLEN HOOPER

My husband won't try anything on, not even shoes. He'll just hold the box up to the light and say, "Yeah, these fit."

—RITA RUDNER

Singing

If birds are such great singers, why don't they put out more albums?

—ELLEN DEGENERES

Single

I'm not good at being alone. Especially at the end of the day when my finances are a mess, my car is falling apart, I can't find my shoe. That's when I need a big, strong guy to hold me close so I can look deep into his eyes and blame him.

—SIMONE ALEXANDER

It bothers me that the world revolves around married people with children, so I've come up with a politically correct term for "single with no kids": happy.

—DANIELLE BROUSSARD

I love New Age jargon. You don't have to admit to being single. You can just say, "I'm learning to be there for myself on a daily basis."

—VANESSA HOLLINGSHEAD

I figure the only time I really need a man is about once a month, when it's time to flip my mattress.

—PAMELA YAGER

The thing I hate about living alone is living alone. I have way too many frivolous conversations with the 411 operator.

—SUE BOVA

I joined a singles group in my neighborhood. The president called me up and asked, "I want to find out what kind of activities you like to plan." I said, "Weddings."

—LYNN HARRIS

Every single one of my friends from high school has long since tied the knot. And I'm getting older; I guess I should think about hanging myself, too.

—LAURA KIGHTLINGER

I'm forty and single. Don't you think it's a generalization that you should be married at forty? That's like looking at somebody who's seventy and saying, "Hey, when are you gonna break your hip? All your friends are breaking their hips—what are you waiting for?"

—SUE KOLINSKY

You know you've been single too long when you call the Jehovah's Witnesses to ask them why they haven't been around lately.

—DEBBIE KASPER

The older you get the lower your standards get. I used to be so picky. "Oh, when I get married he's going to be tall, handsome, rich . . ." and I'm down to: registered voter. I'd marry a midget just for the handicapped parking.

—KATHLEEN MADIGAN

I'm single now and it's really weird for me to be dating again, because the last three years I'd just been cheating.

—AMY BARNES

Why get married and make one man miserable when I can stay single and make thousands miserable?

—CARRIE SNOW

Men don't live well by themselves. They don't even live like people. They live like bears with furniture. I used to go over to my husband's cave. Nothing on the walls, except for some food. The frost was so thick in the freezer you couldn't close the apartment door. The roaches in his kitchen had stopped eating: They were full. They were on the counter doing aerobic exercise.

—RITA RUDNER

Sisters

I'm very insecure and I need a lot of attention because my parents favored my sister. They'd bend over my crib and say, "*Ooh, you have such a cute sister.*"

—KAREN HABER

My little sister Kelly is so cute. She got all my mother's genes. She has a feminine little ski-jump nose, she's naturally skinny, and has no addictions. I got all my father's genes, and I wear them when I'm barhopping to all the places where I can smoke.

—SALLY JACKSON

Skin Care

I'm careful about staying out of the sun. It's so bad for your skin. It makes you leathery and wrinkly and old. Sometimes I see those beautiful sixteen-year-old girls just baking themselves on the beach, and think, "Fry, you home-wreckers, fry!"

—RITA RUDNER

I'm constantly exfoliating. Scrubs, peels, fruit acids, loofahs. My house is full of skin I've deliberately removed. I've started wearing a painter's mask so I don't inhale myself. Because I want to be silky smooth at all times. Silky smooth when I say to that special guy, "Okay, you've had your fun, now get out."

—ROBIN ROBERTS

Sleeping

I'm a sleepaholic. Guys, please don't ask me to sleep with you, because that's exactly what's going to happen.

—LIVIA SQUIRES

I love to sleep. It's the best of both worlds. You get to be alive, and unconscious.

—RITA RUDNER

I decided to take better control of my life and make sure that less things go wrong, so I've been sleeping for twenty hours a day. I figured that in four hours even I couldn't screw up that many things. And if I have to parallel park, that leaves me with just the one hour to kill.

—PAULA POUNDSTONE

I read an article in *Self* magazine that said "drunk sleep" isn't really sleeping. If that's the case, I haven't really slept since high school.

—CHRISTINE O'ROURKE

Slumber Parties

Do you remember when all of your little girlfriends would get together at a slumber party and play with the Ouija board? You'd ask it, "Who am I going to marry? Who am I going to marry? And it would spell out some cute boy's name like, Kevin or Jason, or Satan.

—JOY GOHRING

Smoking

My friends have all quit smoking. I'm such a procrastinator. I can't even seem to start. I think maybe I'll begin with the patch, incessant gum chewing, and then just go hot turkey.

—CYNDI STILES

You nonsmokers are the pissiest people. You're so demanding about your opportunity for clean air space. How can I possibly respect you? You don't have the nerve to take your own life in a horrible way, slowly and painfully, over a great number of years.

—STEPHANIE HODGE

I quit smoking. Now I chew nicotine gum: that last piece of Trident in the bottom of my purse with tobacco stuck all over it. Poor man's Nicorette. I only buy cigarettes to make the gum.

—JAYNE WARREN

I quit smoking. I feel better. I smell better. And it's safer to drink out of old beer cans lying around the house.

—ROSEANNE BARR

Cigarettes should have a label that reads WARNING: QUITTING SMOKING GREATLY INCREASES THE ODDS OF BECOMING INCREDIBLY BITCHY.

—MEL FINE

I finally quit smoking by using the patch. I put six of them over my mouth.

—WENDY LIEBMAN

Snacks

Sometimes when I'm feeling sad or lonely, I'll have a snack, like a brownie or a cupcake, and it makes me feel better. I don't think that's such a big deal, because I know a lot of women who, when they're feeling sad or lonely, will have a baby.

—JESSICA DELFINO

When I buy cookies I just eat four and throw the rest away. But first I spray them with Raid so I won't dig them out of the garbage later. Be careful, though, because Raid really doesn't taste that bad.

—JANETTE BARBER

You want my recipe for trail mix? Plain M&M's, Kraft Caramels, Peanut M&M's. It gets me over the mountain.

—ROSEANNE BARR

Sneezing

This woman sneezed like three hundred times. She said, "There must be something in the air." I said, "Yeah, your germs."

—LINDA HERSKOVIC

Soda

I'm drinking a Diet Coke, because frankly I ate a whole box of Pop-Tarts yesterday and this will take it away.

—PAULA POUNDSTONE

I went out to lunch today and ordered a Dr. Pepper. The waitress said, "We don't have Dr. Pepper, we have Mr. Pibb. It's the same thing." It's not the same thing at all. Dr. Pepper went to school an extra four years. He's much more qualified to be a soft drink. We don't even know if Mr. Pibb has a GED.

—LIVIA SQUIRES

Sororities

I thought when you joined a sorority, they handed you a beer and a frat boy and said, "Go have fun." But when I joined I got a lecture. "This sorority is not about partying and getting drunk. It's about philanthropy and sisterhood." I replied, "I didn't spend my scholarship money on a Brazilian wax to help some old lady cross the street. Now let's go down to South Padre and get our tits on video!"

—DAVA KRAUSE

Being in a sorority was like flying coach. Both had bitchy women telling me all I was allowed to eat was a small bag of pretzels and a diet Coke.

—STEPHANIE SCHIERN

Spanking

I was a mom who did everything by the book. I didn't spank, I used "time-out." That's where you count to ten to allow the Valium to kick in.

—ROBIN FAIRBANKS

I remember the days when it was fashionable to spank your child. My father would say to me, "This hurts me worse than it does you." I wanted to say, "Then you bend over, and I'll lighten your emotional load, buddy."

—LIZ SELLS

I was spanked a few times, and all it did to me was now I like to get spanked.

—SARAH SILVERMAN

Sperm Banks

For a woman the worst thing about a sperm bank is that sperm is no longer free. Just go into a bar, and a sperm container will try to pick you up.

—TINA GEORGIE

I know that some lesbians are getting pregnant by going to sperm banks. I couldn't do that. I'm exactly like my grandmother: "What? Everything's frozen! Nothing's fresh?"

—JUDY CARTER

Sports

If you want a guy to do something for you, all you have to do is introduce an element of senseless danger, and it becomes a sport. "Honey, why don't you try to take out the trash—while I chase you on Rollerblades with a chain saw!"

—C. LYNN MITCHELL

I think sports stars make great role models, particularly if you are thinking about a career in crime.

—LAURA KIGHTLINGER

Every time a baseball player grabs his crotch, it makes him spit. That's why you should never date a baseball player.

—MARSHA WARFIELD

Men own basketball teams. Every year cheerleaders' outfits get tighter and briefer, and players' shorts get baggier and longer.

—RITA RUDNER

Women are now referees for the NBA, and they're driving some guys crazy. They don't just call a foul, they want to talk about why it happened.

—LESLIE NESBITT

You don't have to be in shape to bowl. It's the only sport where there's a way to signal for a cocktail waitress.

—ROBIN ROBERTS

I bowled for two years in college, because I was drunk and needed shoes.

—KATHLEEN MADIGAN

I'm working on letting go. I just can't do it when I'm bungee jumping;
I kinda want to hang on. I love to bungee jump, though. The last time
was over a stream in Canada, a gorgeous place! The problem is: When
I jump, I can't see a thing because my shirt falls down over my head.
The spectators get a better view than I do.

—JOHNNYE JONES GIBSON

Whenever I watch figure skating I don't how these people have the
patience to be with a partner. If I practiced with some guy for ten
years and we got to the Olympics and he fell, I'd skate over to chop
off a finger before he got up. I'd go up to the judges' table and say,
"I don't know who that man is. He's stalking me, and I'd like him
removed from the building. I don't know why his outfit matches mine."

—KATHLEEN MADIGAN

I've been trying to understand men by watching football, and I noticed
that they treat the football like a woman. They hold on to it, they take
it places, and never let it out of their sight. Until the moment they
score, when they toss it aside.

—MAUREEN MURPHY

My husband went to Penn State and during football season, if what I
have to say doesn't start with a national anthem and end with a score,
he can't hear me.

—LAURIE MCDERMOTT

My husband is from England and had never seen a football game before.
So I could tell him anything I wanted. I told him it was over at halftime.

—RITA RUDNER

The reason women don't play football is because eleven of them would
never wear the same outfit in public.

—PHYLLIS DILLER

A male sportscaster disparaged women golfers, saying that breasts get in the way of their swings. Obviously that foot got in the way of his mouth. However, using his logic, men would have a built-in handicap when running track. And let's not talk about the hurdles.

—LEIGHANN LORD

I play on New York City's only women's hockey team. We do play rough. We have checking. The only difference between men's and women's hockey is that women check, but then they apologize.

—LYNN HARRIS

I was in Utah, the land of the Mormons. I didn't see no black people there, but they were real nice and friendly to me. "We like to rock climb. Want to go rock climbing with us?" I was like, "No, I'm black. Black people are not going to gravitate towards a sport where you hang a rope around your body and hang from high places."

—RENÉ HICKS

I played rugby for a while, so I took a break from drinking to get in shape for the rugby season. That's sort of an interesting decision: to stop taking in a painkiller in order to involve myself in a sport that could cause a fair amount of pain.

—SABRINA MATTHEWS

The way a man plays a game can be very revealing. I was playing tennis with a man I had been dating for a while and noticed his reluctance to keep score properly. He couldn't say, "Thirty-love." He kept saying, "Thirty, I really like you but still have to see other people."

—RITA RUDNER

Tennis is like marrying for money. Love has nothing to do with it.

—PHYLLIS DILLER

I don't believe for a second that weightlifting is a sport. They pick up a heavy thing and put it down again. To me, that's indecision.

—PAULA POUNDSTONE

Stains

Happiness is getting a brown gravy stain on a brown dress.

—TOTIE FIELDS

Stocks

I read about a socially responsible stock fund that only invests in companies with a good environmental record and fair labor practices. I assume that by "fair labor practices" they mean one that pays women no less than seventy-nine cents for every dollar they pay men.

—JANINE DITULLIO

I got out of the stock market, and I told my broker, "Hey, put all my money in weed." The price of weed is never going down.

—WANDA SYKES

Stress

I read this article. It said the typical symptoms of stress are eating too much, smoking too much, impulse buying, and driving too fast. Are they kidding? This is my idea of a great day!

—MONICA PIPER

Men, your lives are less stressful. For one thing, what you are wearing now will be in style for the rest of your lives.

—CAROL SISKIND

Strip Clubs

They opened up a strip bar in my neighborhood. Big sign out front, TOTALLY NUDE. I thought they meant to get in. So, I'm standing in line . . .

—MARGARET SMITH

Strippers

One of my friends was getting married, and they tell me I have to chip in for a male stripper. Are you out of your damn mind? I ain't paying for no naked-ass man. Women don't have to pay to see that. We spend most of our time trying *not* to see that.

—WANDA SYKES

My friends hired a male stripper for my birthday present. This guy starts throwing his clothes off and asks me, "What are you thinking, baby?" I'm thinking I've been married too long, because I said, "You're going to pick up after yourself, aren't you?"

—MARY PFEIFFER

The guys at strip clubs put a dollar in the strippers' G-string, sit back down. Put a dollar in, sit down. Two in the morning, they're drunk and say to their friends, "Dude, I'm coming back tomorrow. I think she likes me." Sure she likes you, the way a landlord likes you on the first of the month.

—MONIQUE MARVEZ

Exotic dancers at a San Francisco strip club went on strike, and I had to ask myself, what would strippers chant on a picket line? "They said they'd pay us more, but they lied. We want more to be objectified!"

—NANCY WAITE

The guys in strip clubs think because they got a pocket full of dollars they got the power, but the chicks got the power. They spin around the pole and you guys are hypnotized. That's how I look at a dessert case, but at least I get to eat mine.

—MONIQUE MARVEZ

I was once a stripper. I took off my jewelry and said, "According to Jewish law, I am now naked."

—CHARISSE SAVARIN

Student Loans

I left college owing eighty thousand dollars in student loans. My mom tells me, "Just think of it as a mortgage." Yeah, and I can wallpaper my cardboard box with the interest statements.

—STEPHANIE SCHIERN

Support

The most support I've gotten in my life is from support hose.

—JANICE HEISS

Surrogates

Surrogate mothers make me wonder: When is the right time to ask someone if you can borrow their uterus? Probably not right after you realize you didn't return their lawn mower.

—CYNDI STILES

In this day and age women can have kids for other women through surrogate motherhood. Is this the ultimate favor or what? I think I'm a good friend. I'll help you move. Okay. But whatever comes out of me after nine months, I'm keeping. I don't care if it's a shoe.

—SUE KOLINSKY

The Vatican came down with a new ruling: no surrogate mothers. Good thing they didn't make this rule before Jesus was born.

—ELAYNE BOOSLER

Tanning

Tanning beds are just wrong. Lying there, broasting in your own juices. I think they should make a George Foreman tan bed. Slightly tilted, with a drippings pan at the bottom.

—MEL FINE

Why do women go to tanning salons? What a waste of time and money. Guys only like the white parts, anyway.

—MARGOT BLACK

Tattoos

My daughter has five tattoos! And not one of them says, "Thanks, Mom, for the wonderful job raising me. Sorry about the C-section scar and the massive weight gain."

—UBU (IBME) ZURUB

Tattoos are the hottest thing right now, but I got one thirty years ago. It was a yellow rose of Texas and green leaf, right over my heart. But with age comes sagging, and my little yellow rose of Texas is now down to my waist and looks like a picture of Tony Bennett with liver disease and an elf hat.

—SALLY JACKSON

Couples who get tattooed are the most optimistic people in the world about relationships. I don't want a former lover's name in my phone book, much less his picture on my ass.

—CAROL SISKIND

Taxes

I worked at a grocery store and part of the training was learning which groceries were taxable and which weren't. Generally, anything the government feels is unnecessary or frivolous is taxed. For example, milk and bread aren't taxable, but candy and soda are. Makes sense, until you get to feminine hygiene products. Maxipads aren't taxed, but tampons are. Apparently, the government recognizes your need for basic feminine protection, but all that horseback riding and swimming is gonna cost ya.

—EILEEN KELLY

They call April "tax time" because it's the time of year you feel like tacks are being pounded into you.

—SUNDA CROONQUIST

I just did my taxes, and I'm getting back $150,000. And people say you can't do your own taxes.

—CHANTEL RAE

Teachers

As a teacher it's important to be politically correct. I've learned not to tell a student they're failing my class but rather that they will have another semester in which to get to know me better.

—BONNIE CHEESEMAN

I like a teacher who gives you something to take home to think about besides homework.

—LILY TOMLIN

I used to substitute teach. The worst. I will never forget this second-grade class where I was subbing for a teacher named Susan. All day long these little annoying children would say, "Susan doesn't do it that way. Susan lets us play, Susan gives us gum. Susan is prettier than you." "Oh, really? Susan's dead."

—CATHY LADMAN

English teachers are tough to date. When we first started dating, I lived in New York and she lived in Ohio, and I would write her all these letters. She'd send them back corrected.

—SUZANNE WESTENHOEFER

Teenagers

The only thing I ever said to my parents when I was a teenager was "Hang up, I got it!"

—CAROL LEIFER

This is my diagram of the teenage brain: me, me, me—you, if you can do something for me.

—JANE CONDON

I have a teenage daughter who wants to go to college. But I wonder why I should pay for her education, when she already knows everything.

—SHEILA KAY

The only way I can get my teenager to smile is this game I came up with called "Let's Plan Mommy's Funeral."

—CORY KAHANEY

My teenage daughter has threatened to run away from home. Oh, pinch me, I'm dreaming, let me help you pack. But even if she did run away, I know she'd come back. Just like a bad check: "Insufficient funds."

—SHEILA KAY

Telephone Calls

Men will say, "I'll call you. I'll call you." When they say they're going to call, they don't, and when they say they're not going to come, they do.

—CAROL HENRY

Sage advice? If you're drunk, stay away from the phone. You can't get the answering machine message back.

—JANEANE GAROFALO

I hate phone solicitors. I'd rather get an obscene call; at least they work for themselves.

—MARGARET SMITH

Telephone Numbers

I have a bad memory for phone numbers. But I don't think if you're one digit off, you should get a whole other person. If you're that close, you should at least get someone who knows where they are.

—RITA RUDNER

Men, if you've ever been given a fake phone number, it means you scare women. Basically, it says, "I'd reject you to your face, but I'm afraid that my head would wind up in the garbage and my body in the bay. So here's a phony phone number. Hopefully, you won't figure that out until I've made my escape."

—LORI CHAPMAN

Telephones

Have you heard the latest bad news? The phone company is going to start charging us when we talk to ourselves.

—JANICE HEISS

At the end of every year, I add up the time that I've spent on hold and subtract it from my age. I don't count that time as really living. Sometimes I spend what seems like hours on hold only to be mysteriously disconnected. These times are so disturbing that I feel justified in subtracting not only from my age but also from my weight.

—RITA RUDNER

People are so obsessed with their cell phones they apparently don't want to miss a call, ever. Twice in the past week I've been in a public restroom when the stall next to me starts ringing. Followed by, "Hello?"

—ANDI RHOADS

Telephones were invented to bring us together, and now we have Caller ID, for the ultimate in passive-aggressive behavior.

—SANDRA BERNHARD

Why is it called Caller ID? I'm at home and the phone rings. I look at the phone. "Ugh, it's Ernie. Let voice mail get it." It should be called "Loser ID." Or, "It's My Mother, No Way, ID."

—JENNIFER POST

I always find money in public phones. When I bring a screwdriver along.

—LINDA HERSKOVIC

Television

I don't like to channel surf. You guys like it, don't you? You like to change the channel. We like to change you.

—WENDY LIEBMAN

TV messed me up as a kid. *Bewitched,* one year they just changed Darrins. For months I was walking up to my father going, "*Daddy?* Just checking."

—ROSIE O'DONNELL

I was watching this documentary on a woman who pulled every hair out of her head. I just admire anyone who can finish what they start.

—LAURA KIGHTLINGER

I wanted to show my cooking group an instructional show on TV, so I ordered the Spice Channel. It started out okay. There was a woman baking a cake and then a man came into the picture, and let me just say for the record that I have never seen a cake frosted that way.

—MARY GALLAGHER

The gayest show on TV? Martha Stewart: She's always got the biggest, hugest, screaming nelly boys on. "Today, we'll be talking to Brad, who has been making Christmas tree ornaments for thirty-five years." And Brad will spin into the room, "Thirty-five and a half years, Martha!"

—SUZANNE WESTENHOEFER

I want to go on Dr. Phil but I can't narrow my problems down to one show. "Dear Dr. Phil: I'm a bulimic, bipolar, depressed, disorganized, alcoholic, agoraphobic TV addict with occasional constipation. P.S., I could really use a makeover."

—TRACEY MACDONALD

I'm addicted to religious television. I think it's the best entertainment on TV. Televangelists are to me the proof that God exists and that she has a fantastic sense of humor.

—CATHRYN MICHON

Television preachers say God talks to them. God talks to them and they can only get a show on cable?

—ELAYNE BOOSLER

I have TV talk-show damage. I look at people now and little signs appear underneath their heads. I was at the gas station the other day, looked at the mechanic and instantly saw this title, "Butthead who will overcharge me."

—KATE CLINTON

I'm writing a new sitcom for HBO, *Sex and the Suburbs*. It's about a five-minute show.

—BETH DAVIDOFF

The Tennis Channel debuted this year. Which comes as great news to the rich, fat, white elitists who were growing tired of the Golf Channel.

—MEL FINE

My husband is so confident that when he watches sports on television, he thinks that if he concentrates he can help his team. If the team is in trouble, he coaches the players from our living room, and if they're really in trouble, I have to get off the phone in case they call him.

—RITA RUDNER

I don't care what sport he's watching on TV, my husband says, "C'mon, there's only two minutes left in the game." Those are the longest two minutes in the universe. Where do you get this clock? I'd like one in my bedroom.

—CORY KAHANEY

Temperature

My girlfriend is always cold, I'm always hot. And that is every relationship, gay, straight, whatever. Can't have two hot people together, because they'd burst into flames. Can't have two cold people, because they'd never leave the house. Gotta have two people bitching at each other for the rest of their days about the temperature in the house.

—SUZANNE WESTENHOEFER

Temporary Work

I've owned a temp agency for the last eighteen years. Ironically, I call it "It's Only Temporary." Although I could have called it "So It's Come to This, Has It?"

—MARIA PARKINSON

Why do people always blame the temp when something goes wrong? My stint at Arthur Andersen didn't work out. Big deal, so I shredded a few things. Then there was that Enron assignment. So I'm not a math major, go figure.

—ROBIN BACH

I used to work as a temp a lot. And I think there's something about steady exposure to fluorescent lights that can dissolve every trace of a personality.

—LAURA KIGHTLINGER

Therapy

I'm in therapy now. I used to be in denial. Which is a lot cheaper.

—ROBIN GREENSPAN

I told my mother that I was thinking about seeing a therapist. She thought that was a good idea because she heard they made a lot of money.

—DARLENE HUNT

In my family, everyone is seeing a psychologist, except my mother. She creates the patients.

—STEPHANIE SCHIERN

I've spent a lot of money on therapy, but I can't use it once I get in my parents' house. Yeah, try therapy talk on my family: "Dad, I feel hurt and sad when you come home drunk from deer hunting, after shooting a cow because you mistook it for a twelve-point buck."

—KELLI DUNHAM

Therapy is like a really easy game show where the answer to every question is: "My mom?"

—ROBIN GREENSPAN

I'm seeing a new therapist. The very first day he says, "Before we get started, I want you to know that I work a fifty-minute hour." I figured it out. They need that extra ten minutes to get on the phone and just dish you to all their friends: "Oh my God, she's *crazy*! She's insane. Oh, I gotta go. I got another freak daddy at the door." Fifty-minute hour. But I didn't say anything. At the end of the session, I just handed him a check. And he says, "Excuse me, but this is only for half." And I say, "Oh, I'm sorry, I should have told you earlier. I pay with a fifty-cent dollar." So it all works out even.

—ROBIN GREENSPAN

My therapist always says that you should be friends with someone before you sleep with them. But the truth of the matter is, once you get to know someone, who the hell wants to have sex with them? Yeah, I'm in therapy. What I don't get about therapy is this: If you always pick the wrong person to be in a relationship with, what makes you think you're going to pick any better when you choose your therapist?

—JUDY CARTER

My psychologist was terrible. He couldn't even validate my parking. He said I was sarcastic and in denial. I was like, "Yeah, right."

—WENDY LIEBMAN

I just broke up with my therapist. That was a Freudian slip; he broke up with me.

—WENDY LIEBMAN

It's weird that I have a parent who's a shrink. It's hard to think of my mom solving other people's problems when she's the root of all mine.

—CAROL LEIFER

Tools

Women don't need conventional tools; we'll use anything that's handy. But when pounding a nail, don't use a shoe; shoes cost sixty dollars a pair. A package of frozen hamburger costs six dollars. Use the hamburger.

—JEANNIE DIETZ

My husband has to have every tool ever made. "It's an air compressor. It shoots out air." So does your butt, use that.

—MARYELLEN HOOPER

Towns

My town was so little, when I was a kid we used to play Monopoly on it.

—DONNA JEAN YOUNG

Growing up in a small town, everyone knows your business. Even in math class, the word problems would be about our family. "If there's a 64 percent chance of Kelli's dad drinking two pints of bourbon each day before work, and Kelli's mom is on her third husband and is pregnant with her fourth child, how many years will it take Kelli's family to get off welfare?"

—KELLI DUNHAM

Toys

They have the same toys we had when we were kids. Remember the Easy-Bake Oven? Who thought of that, cooking food on a light bulb? It messed me up when I started to date. "You hungry? It's up on the chandelier. Can you hit the dimmer switch? I think it's burning."

—ROSIE O'DONNELL

I was in McDonald's and I saw this kid take his Happy Meal toy and throw it on the ground. His mom said, "Hey, you play with that. There are children in China manufacturing those."

—LAURA SILVERMAN

My favorite toy was the Crayola sixty-four box. It's like a child's orgasm.

—CATHY LADMAN

Remember Slinky? Minutes of fun! Unfortunately, I grew up living in a one-story house.

—JEANNE WILEY

I'm a subversive. I just began distribution of my new product, "Roadkill Beanie Babies."

—NANCY WAITE

Transvestites

I know my sexuality, but I get so confused by other people's. I don't even know the difference between transvestites and transsexuals. As I understand it, transvestites are the ones that grow down from the ceiling and transsexuals are the ones that grow up.

—PAMELA YAGER

I was dating a transvestite. My mother said, "Marry him, and you'll double your wardrobe."

—JOAN RIVERS

Trauma

I'm suffering from post-post-traumatic syndrome, and I'm going to keep talking about it until some cute guy holds me.

—KATHY GRIFFIN

Trucks

I saw a truck today. Side of the door it said, "Driver has no cash." I'm broke, too. I don't plaster it all over the side of my car.

—MARGARET SMITH

My best friend got a truck. But she didn't want to be trendy, so she got a UPS truck. Laugh, but she can park it anywhere. Worldwide.

—WENDY LIEBMAN

UFOs

UFO sightings are never by anybody intelligent. A UFO has never landed at Harvard or Yale or Princeton. It's always two assholes with Coors beer and a recreational vehicle.

—JOAN RIVERS

I think that's why the aliens don't ever stay; look at the people they meet. Every time they come here they land in the middle of nowhere and meet two guys in overalls with no teeth. "C'mere, you little critters. Earl and me would take you bowling, if you had a couple more fingers on you."

—KATHLEEN MADIGAN

The only thing that scares me more than space aliens is the idea that there aren't any space aliens. We can't be the best that creation has to offer. I pray we're not all there is. If so, we're in big trouble.

—ELLEN DEGENERES

Underwear

When do we put on the lingerie? Always at the beginning of the relationship, right? First couple of months, you know, strutting around the bedroom wearing a teddy. Six months later, you've stopped shaving your legs and you look like a teddy.

—CAROL LEIFER

You don't buy those Victoria's Secret things, do you, you women? Poo! Those things ought to come with a tube of Monistat.

—MARGARET SMITH

My mother buys me these big granny panties, three in a pack. You can use them for a car cover.

—MONIQUE MARVEZ

We got to stick together, big girls. We sexy! We wear thongs now. Oh, yeah. I wear a thong. You may not be able to see it, but I can wear it.

—TESS

I think thong underwear functions better as a sling shot than as a vagina coverall.

—BONNIE CHEESEMAN

Stop buying lingerie, it's a rip-off. Eighteen dollars for a panty this big. One trip through the dryer and it's a frilly bookmark.

—CAROL LEIFER

I'm opening a pair of underwear the other day and a little piece of paper falls out right on the floor. I pick it up. "Inspected by Mary Lou." "Well, thank God," I thought. "That last pair burst into flames. Now that Mary Lou's on the job, I can walk around safe in my underwear."

—MARGARET SMITH

I bought a pair of thong underwear because a friend told me they were comfortable. They're not. Not comfortable for me, and not comfortable for the people watching me dig 'em out of my rear end all night.

—MEL FINE

Why does women's underwear have lace and flowers all over it? You never see men's underwear with a big wrench in the middle of it.

—HEIDI JOYCE

I get attached to my underwear because I'm sentimental. I have one pair full of holes, but they're my lucky underwear, I wore them when I passed the bar exam twelve years ago. John F. Kennedy Jr. failed the bar exam thirteen times. I should have loaned him my underwear. I guess his father, JFK, passed the bar the first time because he was wearing Marilyn Monroe's panties.

—JENNIFER POST

I was out of clean underwear. I had to dig through the drawer for that undie of last resort. Some briefs from the Ming dynasty, with a safety pin. Finally I get all desperate, got a tube sock, some duck tape. I'm a panty MacGyver. Can't find panties, I will make my own.

—AISHA TYLER

Uniforms

Sometimes the police get carried away with those uniforms. I got a ticket for jaywalking and I was petrified. This policeman comes up to me. He has this great big helmet, big black boots, sunglasses, and the belt with all the stuff hanging off it. And he says, "Excuse me, little lady. Did you know you crossed against the light?" I had this terrible desire to say, "No, and do you know that you look like one of the Village People?"

—RITA RUDNER

They say women love a man in uniform. It's true. The uniform sends a clear message: He has a job.

—MIMI GONZALEZ

Vacations

Every year my family would pile into the car for our vacation and drive eighty trillion miles just to prove we couldn't get along in any setting.

—JANEANE GAROFALO

Before going on long trips, I always tell my kids the same thing. "Speak now, or forever hold your pee."

—MEL FINE

My family loves to eat. These are people who go on vacation and come back with slides of the buffet table. They'll only go on cruises, which are moving buffets to them.

—MARIA MENOZZI

I promised some people I'd water their plants and take care of their animals while they're on vacation. They're farmers.

—JANINE DITULLIO

Vacuum Cleaners

For Christmas I got a vacuum cleaner. I was drunk when I assembled it. Now it's an indoor leaf blower.

—SIMONE ALEXANDER

Why do they put lights on vacuum cleaners? To see the dirt? I don't want to see the dirt; that's why I vacuum.

—JEANNIE DIETZ

The day I worry about cleaning my house is the day Sears comes out with a riding vacuum cleaner.

—ROSEANNE BARR

Vegetarians

I'm a vegetarian, but I'm not that hard-core. I eat eggs. I have to, because I'm pro-choice.

—BETSY SALKIND

You know what a hungry vegetarian says? "I'm so hungry I could eat a tree."

—JANICE HEISS

The most self-righteous group today are those damn vegetarians. Your friend feels it's her duty to inform you that you are eating dead flesh. But I prefer it that way. I hate when the flesh moves around on my plate.

—KAREN RIPLEY

I'm not a vegetarian for a few good reasons. First of all, I really love the way meat tastes. But even more important than that, I really, really hate animals, and that's my little way of letting them know.

—JESSICA DELFINO

I was a vegetarian until I started leaning towards sunlight.

—RITA RUDNER

Ventriloquism

My mother was a ventriloquist. She could throw her voice. So for ten years I thought the dog was telling me to kill my father.

—WENDY LIEBMAN

Veterinarians

I have such an expensive vet. I go to pick my dog up and the girl behind the counter says, "Three thousand dollars." The whole waiting room looks up. A woman says, "What happened?" "Well, apparently the dog bought a car after I dropped him off."

—ELAYNE BOOSLER

Viagra

Viagra is the work of the devil. Now we girls can look forward to having sex with really old guys, for a really long time.

—LEMAIRE

Vibrators

To me, sexual freedom meant freedom from having to have sex. And then along came Good Vibrations. As a love object, it surpasses my husband, Harold, by a country mile. But this is not a threat to the family unit. I think of it as a kind of Hamburger Helper for the boudoir.

—LILY TOMLIN

Victoria's Secret

I figured out Victoria's Secret. Starvation and liposuction.

—MEL FINE

Video Games

The news is always going on about how video games are too violent. Sure, there are some video games small children shouldn't play, but I'm a grown woman, and I need to shoot shit. And it's best if that happens fictionally.

—JACKIE KASHIAN

Videos

Yesterday was the thirty-fifth anniversary of the camcorder. It was also the thirty-fifth anniversary of the saying "Come on, baby, I swear nobody will see this but us."

—JENNIFER VALLY

If you buy your husband or boyfriend a video camera, for the first few weeks he has it, lock the door when you go to the bathroom. Most of my husband's early films end with a scream and a flush.

—RITA RUDNER

I used to work at a video store. Part of my job was calling about overdue movies, and gentlemen, let me give you a tip: If you're married and renting porn without your wife's knowledge, bring it back on time. Because this was my job: "Hello, Mrs. Twomey, this is Armonk Video calling about Mr. Twomey's overdue movie, *Genital Hospital*."

—EILEEN KELLY

Virginity

I don't think a woman should be a virgin before marriage. She should have had at least one other disappointing experience.

—MAUREEN MURPHY

I was a virgin until I was twenty. And then again, until I was twenty-three.

—CARRIE SNOW

The most precious gift you can give to a man is your virginity. I ought to know, I've given it to at least a dozen men.

—LIVIA SQUIRES

I used to be a virgin, but I gave it up—there was no money in it.

—MARSHA WARFIELD

Voices

I hate my voice because I don't think it's sexy. I got an obscene phone call, and I actually felt guilty because I thought I turned the guy off.

—CATHY LADMAN

I hear voices in my head. I don't worry about it because that's where my ears are.

—SIMONE ALEXANDER

W, X, Y, Z

Waiters

Waiters are becoming much nicer and more caring.
I used to pay my check, they'd say, "Thank you." That
graduated into, "Have a nice day." That's now escalated
into, "You take care of yourself, now." The other day I
paid my check, the waiter said, "Don't put off that
mammogram."

—RITA RUDNER

Waking Up

I'm amazed at people who wake up by themselves. I have
a friend who says, "The sun wakes me up. I don't need
an alarm." I find that amazing. The only way the sun could
wake me up is if it set me on fire.

—LIVIA SQUIRES

War

If women ruled the world and we all got massages, there would be no war.

—CARRIE SNOW

Men are brave enough to go to war, but they are not brave enough to get a bikini wax.

—RITA RUDNER

Weaponry

LG-118 Peacekeeper missile. Doesn't that sound like Ax-murderer Baby-sitter?

—ELAYNE BOOSLER

Wedding Ring

I like a man who wears a wedding ring. Because without it, they're like a shark without a fin. You pretty much got to know they're out there.

—BRETT BUTLER

My husband, Fang, was the cheapest man alive. My wedding ring turned my whole body green. My engagement ring, he said it was a square-cut emerald, it was a Chiclet.

—PHYLLIS DILLER

Weddings

Once you're in a relationship, everybody wants to know, "When's the wedding, when's the wedding?" I'm on to them. They're only asking because they want a party. Why should my life be ruined just because you want to get smashed and eat cake? There's a bakery and a liquor store in every town. You can become a fat alcoholic on your own; leave me out of it.

—LEE ARLETH

I dated my husband for three years. I thought if he doesn't propose soon, I'm throwing him a surprise wedding. He would walk in, and everyone would shout, "Surprise!" Then I would say, "Honey, have you met Father Marconi? Oh, someone just asked, 'Who wants to go fishing?' Honey, say '*I do.*'"

—FRANCES DILORINZO

Skimp on your wedding dress. Why spend a lot of money on something you're only going to wear five or six times?

—CHARISSE SAVARIN

On her wedding day, a Masai tribeswoman symbolizes her low status by putting dung on her head. American women may have to put up with a lot of bullshit, but at least we don't have to wear it.

—JACKIE WOLLNER

I had a civil ceremony. His mother couldn't come.

—PHYLLIS DILLER

My husband and I had a really nice wedding. We have a mixed marriage. I'm Jewish, and he ain't. For my family, he crushed a beer can under his foot. For his family, I pretended I was a virgin.

—ROSEANNE BARR

I love weddings, but I cry. Because they're not mine.

—WENDY LIEBMAN

I was invited to a gay wedding. I caught the jockstrap.

—PHYLLIS DILLER

Caucasians do things differently at their weddings than Mexicans do. Like, they send out invitations. Ahead of time. See, we pull up to the corner, "Hey, Chuy! My cousin Carlos is getting married. Follow me!"

—DEBI GUTIERREZ

My wedding night was a disaster. My husband tried to get the garter off over my head.

—PHYLLIS DILLER

Weight

I had this boyfriend who told me he thought I needed to lose weight. He really hurt my feelings, but he was right. I'm proud to say I lost 173 pounds, when I dumped him. I can't tell you how much better I feel.

—WENDY KAMENOFF

I'm trying to get back to my original weight—eight pounds, three ounces.

—CHERIL VENDETTI

I'm not fat, I'm just short for my weight. I should be nine-seven.

—TOTIE FIELDS

Hollywood says I'm overweight and I don't give a damn. I'm a hottie, I don't care what they say. I think the only thing that should be ninety pounds is one full-grown, voluptuous breast.

—TESS

I'm not fat, I'm just too big for my head.

—DEBBIE KASPER

I don't have a fat body, I just have a really big head. I don't know how I'm going to lose weight in my head. What kind of crunches do I have to do?

—MARGARET CHO

Too many women trying to be super-thin. I went to a party the other night, a model walked by me and I got a paper cut.

—LEMAIRE

I have several girlfriends who are constantly watching their weight. Even at forty- and fifty-something, they down skinny cappuccinos, fat-free chocolate puddings, and low-fat chocolate cookies. Girls, there are some things you should fake, but chocolate isn't one of them.

—JACKIE NEWTON

Men date thin girls because they're too weak to argue and salads are cheap.

—JENNIFER FAIRBANKS

I realized when I got a little older that women are skinny for other women. Men don't care. Men will screw mud. "It's warm, it's wet; I'm going in."

—MONIQUE MARVEZ

I wonder if men with beer bellies know that they're fat? Because they cinch the belt *under* their stomachs, so they're still wearing the 32 belt, right? But their actual stomach is 60. So do these guys think they've still got a waist, and they're just hiding several small human children under their shirts?

—ROSIE TRAN

I can't stand these anorexic fashion sluts who whine, "I eat and eat, and I can never put on weight." Well, just lay down and I'll drop the UN building on you. That ought to pack on the pounds.

—JUDY TENUTA

I read that in the first year of marriage the average man gains nineteen and a half pounds. The average woman twenty-seven. Great. I'm not only gaining weight, I'm gaining a fat guy.

—KRIS MCGAHA

I'm starting to gain a little weight because you live with a man, you gain weight. You know why? You starved your whole life to get one; you got one, you're going to eat now.

—ELAYNE BOOSLER

A recent study conducted by the American Medical Association shows that sleep loss may be linked to weight gain. So the next time someone asks if you've put on a few pounds, say, "No, my husband snores."

—CAROLINE RHEA

My husband and I both gained weight after we got married, and so we went on a diet together. He lost weight, and I didn't. I had to feed him in his sleep, intravenously.

—RITA RUDNER

You gain over fifty pounds, everything changes. You put on your underwear and they explode. I've got workmen at my house scraping the underwear shrapnel off of the walls.

—MEG MALY

My mother wanted me to go with her to a fat farm. She calls it a fat farm, but you can't exactly grow fat there, unless you tip the kitchen staff.

—CARRIE SNOW

It's hard to be famous and struggle with a weight problem. I was in Baskin-Robbins, just looking, and this lady said to me, "Are you Rosie O'Donnell?" I said, "Yes." "I didn't know you were pregnant." I looked at her and said, "Yes, four and a half months." She kept asking. "What are you going to name it?" "I don't know, either Ben or Jerry."

—ROSIE O'DONNELL

Girls, do you retain water? I retain pizzas and Twinkies.

—ETTA MAY

The state of Maine is planning to pass anti-obesity legislation. I go there every summer. I can hear it now, "Miss, you're about two candy bars away from a felony."

—CAROLINE RHEA

You know you're getting fat when you get in the bathtub and the water in the toilet goes up.

—ETTA MAY

White Trash

I think of myself lovingly as white trailer trash. My parents recently made up their will. Everything is split equally between me and my sister. She's getting the house, but I'm getting the porch and the wheels.

—LYNDA MONTGOMERY

Wives

Wives are people who think it's against the law not to answer the phone when it rings.

—RITA RUDNER

People ask, "Are you a good cook?" No, but I'm a great wife. I married my Georgie, the first day I said, "Pick out which room in the house you want me to be great in." Thank God, he goes out to eat a lot.

—TOTIE FIELDS

Women

Women, we've got to be kinder to each other. I've given it a lot of thought. Let's be honest, there's not a man in this world who couldn't be replaced by a winning lotto ticket and a Water Pik.

—MONIQUE MARVEZ

We're our own worst enemies a lot of the time, but I still blame men.

—JANEANE GAROFALO

A new survey shows that the more female you are physically, the harder it is to be taken seriously in business. For example, women with very large breasts have a harder time being promoted than women with penises.

—HEIDI JOYCE

The thing women have yet to learn is nobody gives you power. You just take it.

—ROSEANNE BARR

Freud accused women of having penis envy. I have no reason to be jealous of a penis. At least when I get out of the ocean, all my bodily parts are still the same size.

—SHEILA WENZ

When women are depressed they eat or go shopping. Men invade another country. It's a whole different way of thinking.

—ELAYNE BOOSLER

Women might start a rumor, but not a war.

—MARGA GOMEZ

Some say it's what's on the inside that counts. If that were true about women, *Playboy* would be running centerfolds of brain tissues and gall bladders.

—CHRISTY MURPHY

All women want from men is a partner who will share his hopes, his thoughts, his dreams. And if you don't, we're going to bitch at you until the day you die.

—STEPHANIE HODGE

Men say women are too emotional and should be more like them. So I guess the next time I get my heart broken instead of crying and eating a pint of Häagen-Dazs, I should drive recklessly to the nearest bar, get my nose broken, and spend the night in jail, because some guy was *lookin' at me!*

—KELLY MAGUIRE

Most women are introspective: "Am I in love? Am I emotionally and creatively fulfilled?" Most men are out-rospective: "Did my team win? How's my car?"

—RITA RUDNER

Why are *we* wearing makeup? I know a few butt-ugly guys who wouldn't be hurt by a little lip color.

—SUE MURPHY

A woman's a woman until the day she dies, but a man's only a man as long as he can.

—MOMS MABLEY

Work

I get to work on time every day, 8:45 A.M. Because the UPS man comes at nine, and he's fine as hell.

—LONI LOVE

I used to work in an office. They're always so mean to the new girl in the office. "Oh, Caroline, you're new? You have lunch at nine-thirty."

—CAROLINE RHEA

Women in the workplace, we still have big strides. Girlfriend of mine just got a new job. First question the new boss asked her was if she could make a good cup of coffee. She stormed right out of that Starbucks.

—CAROL LEIFER

I was a secretary. And like a lot of secretaries, I practically ran that company. Into the ground.

—WENDY LIEBMAN

When I worked in the computer industry, people often referred to me as a "female executive." Is that necessary? I prefer the more politically correct "salary-impaired."

—JACKIE WOLLNER

I had the meanest boss in the world, so I would call in sick a lot. I would say I had "female problems." My boss didn't know I meant her.

—WENDY LIEBMAN

Are you ever at work and your boss is telling you how to spell your name, and you're clutching a pen in your hand as tightly as Bob Dole. And you think, "I will not drive this into his skull, I will not drive this into his skull." You could change jobs but it wouldn't really matter. Same assholes, different pens.

—JANET ROSEN

Never take a job where the boss calls you "babe."

—BRETT BUTLER

I worked as a receptionist, but I couldn't get the hang of it. I answered the phone, "Hello. Can you help me?"

—CAROLINE RHEA

I used to work at the International House of Pancakes. People complained all the time about the service. We weren't slow, the floors were sticky. We were stuck in the back trying to get to the tables.

—PAULA POUNDSTONE

The trouble with being in the rat race is that even if you win, you're still a rat.

—LILY TOMLIN

World

I once wanted to save the world, now I just want to leave the room with some dignity.

—LOTUS WEINSTOCK

Writing

I'm a writer. I write checks. Mostly fiction.

—WENDY LIEBMAN

Yoga

I enjoy yoga. I enjoy any exercise where you get to lie down on the floor and go to sleep.

—RITA RUDNER

I feel weird in yoga with my legs over my shoulders and my behind over my face, and the guy on the mat next to me says, "Haven't I seen you someplace?"

—MAUREEN MURPHY

They say that yoga is a great way to use your body to reach a higher consciousness. I find it's a lot easier just to drink, to get your legs behind your neck like that.

—WENDY LIEBMAN

Younger Men

I think women should date younger men. Thirty-five-, forty-year-old women are peaking when eighteen-year-old boys are peaking, and that's who we should be peaking and poking.

—SHEILA KAY

W, X, Y, Z

Do you know how hard it is to have sex with these little eighteen-year-old boys with your foot up against the door so his strong-ass mama don't bust in on you? And then when she busts in on you, the only thing you can think to say is, "Hey, didn't we go to high school together?"

—SHERYL UNDERWOOD

The younger men, all right! They still come too quick and go to sleep right after, but they can do it every goddamn night.

—ROSEANNE BARR

Younger guys have been approaching me lately. And asking me to buy them alcohol.

—WENDY LIEBMAN

I've been dating this nineteen-year-old. We were getting hot and heavy the other night, but he was just fumbling around. I thought I should try to communicate with him in a manner he'd understand, so I whispered into his ear, "You have reached Level Five, you may now enter the cave."

—JOY GOHRING

I'm dating a guy who's twenty-one. That's seven in boy years.

—LISA GOICH

When I was single I used to date younger men. Until I realized: Skateboarding is not a career option.

—BETH DAVIDOFF

I married a younger man. Five years younger than I am. I figure it like this: If you can't find a good man, raise one.

—WANDA SYKES

Zoos

I went to the zoo this weekend and saw a lot of things. For instance, I observed that if you need a beer at two in the afternoon to take your sons to the zoo, you've got bigger fish to fry than the ex-wife only letting you have the kids every other weekend.

—WENDY WILKINS

When I was growing up, we had a petting zoo and, well, we had two sections. We had a petting zoo, and then we had a heavy-petting zoo. For people who really liked the animals a lot.

—ELLEN DEGENERES

Green Room

Natasha Ahanin is an actress and stand-up comedian who has performed at the Comedy Store in Hollywood.

Simone Alexander is a San Francisco-based stand-up comedian and contributing writer to laugh.com. Contact: quofacit@aol.com.

Gracie Allen was a classic comedienne whose career ranged from vaudeville and movies to the 1950s sitcom *Burns & Allen*.

Lee Arleth is a stand-up comic from New Jersey. She is also a well-known masochist, as she refuses to date anyone but other comedians. This qualifies her for all the free antidepressants she can swallow at the local clinic.

Amy Ashton is a model turned actress, who then turned comedian when she grew tired of being stereotyped as either a bimbo or a bitch.

Comedian **Leah Krinsky Atkins** has been an Emmy–award-winning writer for HBO's *Dennis Miller Show.*

Comedian **Karen Babbitt** teaches acting and stand-up at San Jose State University.

Robin Bach dove into the stand-up arena at the age of forty and has since performed at Zanies in Chicago, the Funny Bone in Columbus, Ohio, and the Comedy Zone in Charlotte, North Carolina, among other clubs.

Michele Balan has appeared on Comedy Central, USA Network, and Lifetime TV. Check her out at michelebalan.com.

In addition to her own Comedy Central special, **Maria Bamford** has appeared on *The Tonight Show* and in the movie *Stuart Little 2.* Check her out at mariabamford.com.

Comedian **Janette Barber** has been a staff writer for *The Rosie O'Donnell Show* and is the author of the humor book *Breaking the Rules: Last-Ditch Tactics for Landing the Man of Your Dreams.*

Vicki Barbolak won California's Funniest Female Competition and has been featured as a *Jenny Jones Show* Comedy Diva. Vicki lives in a trailer in Vista, California, with her two daughters and dog Sparky, who bears an amazing resemblance to Suzanne Somers.

Susie Barker is a stand-up comedian who hails from Pittsburgh, Pennsylvania. Contact: susiemeister@hotmail.com.

Amy Barnes has been featured on Comedy Central's *Premium Blend.*

Roseanne Barr is the comedian who has specialized in eponymous TV such as *Roseanne,* the sitcom, *The Roseanne Show,* a talk show, and *The Real Roseanne Show.*

Comedian **Rhonda Bates** has appeared on the TV shows *Vegas* and *The Love Boat.*

Shari Becker has performed at the Comedy Store and the Ice House in Los Angeles, as well as other comedy clubs, and she has appeared in many radio and TV commercials. Check her out at occomedy.com/bio/becker/becker.htm.

Elizabeth Beckwith has appeared on Comedy Central's *Premium Blend* and in the movie *Coyote Ugly.*

Joy Behar is a comedian and actress who serves as comic relief on the ABC daytime talk show *The View.*

Comedian **Paula Bell** has appeared on the *Tonight Show* with Jay Leno.

Comedian **Suzy Berger** has appeared at the Montreal Comedy Festival, and her material has been featured in the book *A Funny Time to Be Gay.*

Karen Bergreen has appeared on Comedy Central's *Premium Blend.*

Comedian **Sandra Bernhard** costarred on *Roseanne* and has starred in a number of films including *The King of Comedy.*

Margot Black is a writer, producer, and stand-up whose credits include MTV's *Jenny McCarthy Show* and *Late Night with David Letterman.*

Christine Blackburn is cohost of "Thursday Night Funnies" at the Comedy Store in Hollywood and has appeared in more than sixty national commercials and infomericals. Say hi at Peaceburn@aol.com.

Comedian **Elayne Boosler** has starred in her own HBO and Showtime specials, including *Party of One.* Check her out at elayneboosler.com.

Jodi Borrello has performed at the House of Blues and the New Orleans Comedy Festival. Check her out at runningfunny.com.

Comedian **Sue Bova** has appeared on NBC's *Homicide,* and in the movies *Absolute Power, Home for the Holidays,* and *Twelve Monkeys.*

Alicia Brandt is a stand-up comedian and an actress who has appeared in a range of roles from *General Hospital* to the movie *Mousehunt.*

Shelley Brigman is a stand-up comic and journalist based in Montgomery, Alabama. Check her out at shelleybrigman.com.

Joanna Briley is a New York–based stand-up comedian. Check her out at comedienneonabudget.com.

Gloria Brinkworth is a psychologist and stand-up comedian who has performed at the Comedy Store.

Danielle Broussard has performed on *Late Night with Conan O'Brien* and has appeared on NBC's *Last Comic Standing*. Check her out at eastcoastcomedy.com/Danielle.htm.

Judy Brown is the editor of the books *Joke Soup, Joke Stew, The Funny Pages,* and *Jokes to Go.*

Comedian **Julie Brown** wrote and performed in the movies *Earth Girls Are Easy* and *Clueless* and the Comedy Central series *Strip Mall.* Check her out at juliebrown.com.

Maureen Brownsey is a comedian and filmmaker. Her films include *True Blue.*

Comedian **Kathy Buckley** is a motivational speaker and winner of an American Comedy Award. Check her out at kathybuckley.com.

Comedian **Brett Butler** is the star of the now-syndicated sitcom *Grace under Fire.* Check her out at brettbutler.com.

Melanie Camacho has appeared on Comedy Central's *Premium Blend* and in the movie *Money Talks.*

Nikki Carr has appeared on BET's *Comic View* and *Showtime at the Apollo.*

Bea Carroll is a singer-songwriter and comedian who has appeared at the Comedy Store, the Jazz Bakery, and the Cinegrill.

Jean Carroll, a classic comedienne of the 1950s and 1960s, appeared on *The Ed Sullivan Show* and many other TV programs of the period, and released a comedy record, *Girl in a Hot Steam Bath.*

Judy Carter is the author of *The Comedy Bible* but bills herself as "just another Jewish lesbian comic-magician." Check her out at judycarter.com.

Tamara Castle is an actress and comedian who has appeared on Comedy Central, *The Tonight Show,* and in the *Pirates of the Caribbean* movie.

Lori Chapman has been performing stand-up comedy for the past four years all over the West Coast, from Seattle to San Diego. She's also single, and, at this point, she's willing to settle for less.

Bonnie Cheeseman does stand-up comedy because it beats sit-down sulking.

Fran Chernowsky is a freelance paralegal and stand-up comedian.

Comedian **Margaret Cho** is a comedy diva and star of her own stand-up films *I'm the One that I Want, Notorious C.H.O.,* and *Revolution.* Check her out at margaretcho.com.

Ellen Cleghorne has been a featured player on *Saturday Night Live* and her own WB series, *Cleghorne.*

Kate Clinton is a groundbreaking lesbian stand-up comedian whose career spans three decades and whose comedy albums include *Babes in Joyland* and *Read My Lips.* Check her out at kateclinton.com.

When she made her stand-up comedy debut at the age of thirteen at the Hollywood Improv in 1999, **Kaitlin Colombo** was introduced as "The Lolita of Laughter, the Jailbait of Stand-up." Kaitlin strutted to the stage, grabbed the microphone, and retorted, "I prefer to think of myself as 'The Amy Fisher of Funny.'"

Jane Condon has been called "the J.Crew mother of two" by *The New York Daily News* and "an upper-crust Roseanne" by the Associated Press. Check her out at janecondon.com.

Sue Costello has appeared on *Tough Crowd with Colin Quinn* and been featured on Comedy Central's *Premium Blend.* Check her out at suecostello.com.

Aurora Cotsbeck is an Australian actress and comedian who has also appeared on the TV series *Stingers* and *Neighbors*.

Eileen Courtney is a former TV technical director, comedian, and current full-time mom who is always funny—and needs to be to keep her sanity.

Sunda Croonquist is a wife and mother of two daughters, and she has performed on Comedy Central, VH-1, HBO, Showtime, and Lifetime Television's *Strong Medicine*.

Courtney Cronin has been seen on HBO's *Curb Your Enthusiasm* and as a featured writer and performer on ESPN's *Mohr Sports*.

Christine Crosby is a Canadian comedian who performs at Yuk Yuk's and other venues.

Sara Cytron has been featured in the PBS lesbian and gay series *In the Life* and in the book *Out Loud & Laughing*.

Beth Davidoff is a stand-up comedian, writer, and stay-at-home mom who lives in Las Vegas. Check her out at comedy.com/bethd.

Comedian **JoAnn Dearing** has appeared on *Evening at the Improv*, Showtime's *Comedy Club Network*, and *Girls' Night Out*.

Comedian **Ellen DeGeneres** is the groundbreaking comedian and star of ABC's *Ellen*, who has been featured in movies that include *Love Letters* and *Mr. Wrong*, and on her own new talk show.

Lea DeLaria hosted Comedy Central's *Out There* and has appeared on Broadway in *On the Town* and *The Most Fabulous Story Ever Told*.

Jessica Delfino has been a finalist on ABC *Good Morning America*'s "Make Us Laugh All Night Long" competition and a writer for the MTV show *I Bet You Will*. Check her out at jessydelfino.blogspot.com.

In addition to performing stand-up, **Susan DePhillips** is a screenwriter who is completing her first nonfiction book and is a stand-up comedy instructor at the Hyena Comedy Institute in San Francisco.

Sully Diaz has appeared on the TV shows *Ellen* and *Culture Clash* and is featured on the CD *Hot and Spicy Mamitas.*

Kathie Dice, a comedian, wife, mother, and hairdresser—to boot—has also written and performed her own one-woman show, a humorous look at the life of the Virgin Mary. Check her out at kjthedj.homestead.com/mary.html.

Jeannie Dietz has written material for Joan Rivers that then was performed on *The Tonight Show.*

Phyllis Diller is a classic comedian who has appeared in a number of movies and on dozens of TV shows over five decades including *The Tonight Show.*

Frances Dilorinzo has appeared on Comedy Central and in USO tours around the world. Check her out at francesd.com.

Comedian **Janine DiTullio** has been a staff writer for *Late Night with Conan O'Brien* and *The Jon Stewart Show.*

Becky Donohue has been featured on Comedy Central's *Premium Blend.*

Beth Donahue, comedian and host of Nashville WKDF morning radio, is the author of the humor book *This Is Insanity! No Dieting, No Exercising, No Counseling, No Results: Stay the Way You Look and Feel—Forever.* Check her out at bethdonahue.com

By day **Kelli Dunham** is a public health nurse, but by night she's a stand-up comedian and award-winning author. Check out this ex-nun on the run at kellidunham.com

Lynn Epstein is a California comedian who has appeared at the Comedy Store and the Improv in Hollywood. Check her out at home.earthlink.net/~lynnsfunny/.

Leah Eva is a San Francisco–based stand-up comedian who tells us she also hopes be the first Filipina-American to have more shoes than Imelda Marcos. Contact: princessleahsf@yahoo.com.

Jennifer Fairbanks has performed on UPN's *Vibe* and is a member of the comedy troupe Fresh Meat, an award-winning San Francisco improv group.

Robin Fairbanks is a Seattle-based stand-up comedian who has opened for comedians Ralph Harris, Sue Murphy, and Bobby Slayton. Robin is also a contributing writer and cast member of the sketch show *The Night Shift* and has appeared in local and national commercials. Check her out at robinfairbanks.com.

Totie Fields was one of the top women comedians in the 1960s, and her television appearances included *The Ed Sullivan Show* and *The Tonight Show.*

Mel Fine is a working comedian throughout the Midwest and the winner of the Indianapolis Funniest Person Contest.

Erin Foley has appeared on Comedy Central's *Premium Blend* and in the motion picture *Almost Famous.*

Diane Ford has received eight nominations for an American Comedy Award. Her HBO specials are classics.

Catherine Franco has played leading ladies in heavy theatrical shows such as *Extremities* and *Children of a Lesser God,* played home-wrecking bitches in a dozen soap operas, and now performs in comedy clubs that include the Laugh Factory in Los Angeles. Contact: cbocaloca@aol.com.

Caryl Fuller's book and solo show, *Dueling Hearts,* is a comic tour de force about charming men and the roller coaster ride of romance. Contact: carylfuller@aol.com.

Mary Gallagher is an actress and comedian whose television credits include *Friends* and *The Tonight Show.* Check her out at marygallagher.tv.

Janeane Garofalo is the queen of the alternative comedians and an actress who has appeared in films that include *The Truth about Cats and Dogs* and *Mystery Men.*

Comedian **Emmy Gay** has appeared at the Apollo Theater and the Joseph Papp Public Theater. Check her out at emmygay.com.

Comedian **Tina Georgie** has appeared on *The Late Late Show with Craig Kilborn.*

Lori Giarnella is a newcomer to the comedy scene in her hometown of Pittsburgh. When she isn't hitting open-mic nights, she masquerades as assistant director of admission and publications coordinator at her alma mater, Carnegie Mellon University.

Johnnye Jones Gibson works for a newspaper, freelances as a journalist, writes screenplays, and travels the world interviewing and writing newsletters for Anthony Robbins Seminars and other events.

Joy Gohring has appeared on Comedy Central and *The Late Late Show with Craig Kilborn.*

Lisa Goich is a stand-up comedian, talk-radio host, award-winning copywriter, and author of the book *The Breakup Diary.*

Judy Gold has appeared on HBO's *Comic Relief,* and *The Tonight Show with Jay Leno* and has starred in her own Comedy Central special. Check her out at jwen.com/jg/index2.asp.

Comedian **Whoopi Goldberg** is the Oscar-winning actress of the film *Ghost,* is cohost of HBO's *Comic Relief,* and has hosted the Oscars and *Hollywood Squares.*

Marga Gomez has appeared on HBO's *Comic Relief,* Showtime's *Latino Laugh Festival,* and Comedy Central's *Out There* special. Check her out at margagomez.com.

Mimi Gonzalez produced the weekly stand-up show *Women with Balls* for six years in Los Angeles and San Francisco. Mimi has also performed comedy from Wenatchee to Biloxi to Tallahassee to Albany and counts entertaining the troops in Japan, Korea, Bosnia, and Kosovo as some of her most rewarding work. Check her out at mimigonzalez.com.

Author and comedian **Debbie Sue Goodman** performs a one-woman show based on her humorous book, *Still Single*. Check her out at stillsingle.org.

Monica Grant is one of the hottest tickets on the women's concert circuit.

Comedian **Robin Greenspan** has been featured on Comedy Central's *Out There in Hollywood* and produced her own CD, *Totally Naked.*

Comedian **E. L. Greggory** is a regular at the Comedy Store in Hollywood.

Comedian **Kathy Griffin** has been featured in the sitcom *Suddenly Susan* and movies *The Cable Guy* and *Pulp Fiction.*

Debi Gutierrez has appeared on Lifetime, Showtime, ABC's *Laughin' Out Loud,* at the Just for Laughs Comedy Festival in Montreal, and at the U.S. Comedy Arts Festival in Aspen, Colorado. Check her out at mommycomic.com.

Comedian **Karen Haber** has been featured on *The Arsenio Hall Show* and *Evening at the Improv* and in the video *The Girls of the Comedy Store.*

Comedian **Rhonda Hansome** has opened for James Brown, the Pointer Sisters, and Anita Baker and appeared in the film *Pretty Woman.*

Comedian **Lynn Harris** has written for *The New York Times* and *Entertainment Weekly* and has created breakupgirl.net and three resulting books, including *Breakup Girl to the Rescue!*

Paulara R. Hawkins has been a semifinalist in Comedy Central's Laugh Riot Competition and featured as one of the Comedians to Watch on *The Jenny Jones Show.* Check her out at artistwebsite.com/paularapage.html.

Laura Hayden has been featured at the Boston International Comedy Festival and has been a semifinalist in the California's Funniest Female Contest. Check her out at laurahayden.com.

Susan Healy is a Los Angeles–based comedian.

Janice Heiss is comedian and member of the San Francisco theater group The Plutonium Players. Her writing has also appeared in the literary magazine *Passages North* and the books *Herotica 2* and *The Ecstatic Moment: the Best of Libido.*

Comedian **Carol Henry** has been featured in HBO's *Women of the Night III.*

Linda Herskovic toured the country as one-half of the comedy team Two Consenting Adults and has contributed to the Shescape literary Web 'zine.

René Hicks starred in her own Comedy Central special, appeared in the movie *Low Down Dirty Shame,* and has been nominated for an American Comedy Award.

Comedian **Stephanie Hodge** starred in the syndicated sitcom *Unhappily Ever After.*

Daryl Hogue is a comedian and voiceover talent whose clients include 7-Eleven, Ford, and Hewlett-Packard. She performs in clubs in the L. A. area.

Vanessa Hollingshead has appeared on Comedy Central's *Tough Crowd with Colin Quinn* and nearly two dozen other TV shows.

Maryellen Hooper won an American Comedy Award, and her numerous television appearances include *The Tonight Show with Jay Leno* and her own Comedy Central special. Check her out at maryellenhooper.com.

Alex House has appeared on *Last Comic Standing* and *The View* and has twice won the Bud Light Ladies of Laughter contest. Check her out at comedy.com/alexhouse.

Sharon Houston has appeared on Comedy Central's *Premium Blend.* Check her out at comedy.com/sharonhouston.

Comedian **Darlene Hunt** has written for the sitcom *Good Morning, Miami* and costarred on *Will & Grace.*

Shannon Ireland is a comedian based in Bloomington, Indiana, who performs at midwestern comedy clubs, church groups, hospital auxiliary banquets, homeless kitchen holiday dinners, and anywhere else that will have her.

Christina Irene has dreamed of becoming a professional writer since she was seven years old, and her comedy career is a fulfillment of that dream. Check her out at christinairene.com.

Sally Jackson's love of the entertainment industry has her heavily involved in casting for major motion pictures, coaching actors, doing coverage on film scripts for one of the biggest producers in Hollywood, and, of course, writing and performing her stand-up at venues in Los Angeles.

Jenée has performed stand-up around the globe, including USO tours of Korea, Bosnia, and Kosovo. Jenée is also a regular contributor to *US Magazine*'s Fashion Police. Check her out at jenee.net.

Geri Jewell has appeared on *Girls' Night Out* and *Comic Strip Live* and was a recurring character on the sitcom *The Facts of Life.*

Comedian **Jenny Jones** is the host of *The Jenny Jones Show.*

Comedian **Diana Jordan** has been nominated for an American Comedy Award, has appeared in the movie *Jerry Maguire,* and is the author of the book *Women Are from Venus, Men Are from Uranus.* Check her out at dianajordan.com

Comedian **Heidi Joyce** is the creator, host, and executive producer of the nationally recognized *Comedy Stand Up against Domestic Violence* CDs on Uproar Entertainment. Heidi also has been featured on *Everybody Loves Raymond*'s "Ray Day" on CBS. Check her out at members.aol.com/comedygrrl.

Tere Joyce has been one of the finalists on NBC's *Last Comic Standing.*

Cory Kahaney has been a finalist on NBC's *Last Comic Standing* and has appeared on Lifetime's *Girls' Night Out,* NBC's *Comedy Showcase,* and Comedy Central.

Wendy Kamenoff is an actress, stand-up comedian, playwright, and mother of seven-year-old Griffin. Her recent TV appearances include HBO's *Curb Your Enthusiasm, The Bernie Mac Show,* and National Lampoon's *Funny Money.* Wendy's company, Parents with Punchlines, produces comedy fund-raisers for private and public elementary schools. Contact: wendykamenoff@aol.com.

Comedian **Kathleen Kanz** lives in Vermont, where everybody's funny, but they don't know it. Contact: kathleenkanz@yahoo.com.

Randy Kaplan has appeared on NBC's *Last Comic Standing.*

Jann Karam has appeared on *Politically Incorrect, The Tonight Show with Jay Leno, Evening at the Improv,* and Lifetime's *Girls' Night Out.* Check her out at jannkaram.com.

Sari Karplus is a Los Angeles–based stand-up comedian who has performed at the Improv and the Knitting Factory, and trained in improvisation and sketch comedy at the Second City and Improv Olympic in Los Angeles. Check her out at sariweb.com.

Jackie Kashian has appeared on A&E's *Comedy on the Road* and at HBO's U.S. Comedy Arts Festival. Check her out at jackiekashian.com.

Comedian **Debbie Kasper** has been a staff writer on the sitcom *Roseanne* and *The Rosie O'Donnell Show,* for which she received two Emmy nominations. Debbie is currently touring with cowriter Sheila Kay in *Venus Attacks,* a comedy about love, sex, and self-help. Check her out at venusattacks.org.

Sheila Kay has been nominated twice for an American Comedy Award and has appeared on the TV Shows *Beverly Hills 90210* and *Murder One.* Check her out at sheilakay.com.

Eileen Kelly is a New York–based stand-up comedian and head writer of the sketch troupe Hits Like a Girl. Check her out at hitslikeagirl.com

Martha Kelly has appeared on Comedy Central and NBC's *Last Comic Standing.*

Jen Kerwin has appeared on NBC's *Last Comic Standing*.

Comedian **Julie Kidd** has been featured on NBC's *Power of Laughter* and on ABC's *The View*, where Joy Behar said of her, "Julie Kidd is one of the funniest housewives in America!" Check her out at funnysinglemom.com.

In addition to being comedy's reigning Queen of Sardonica, **Laura Kightlinger** is a writer and producer of the sitcom *Will & Grace*.

Comedian **Karen Kilgariff** is the head writer of *The Ellen DeGeneres Show* and has appeared on HBO's *Mr. Show* and *The Drew Carey Show*.

Tina Kim has appeared on of NBC's *Last Comic Standing*. Check her out at tinakim.com.

Dani Klein is a comedian and actor who has appeared on *Law & Order* and in the movie remake of *The Out-of-Towners*.

Comedian **Sue Kolinsky** has performed on *The Tonight Show* and her own Comedy Central special.

After graduating Northwestern University in 2001, **Dava Krause** moved to Los Angeles, where she has become a regular performer at the Comedy Store.

Elvira Kurt starred in her very own Comedy Central special and released her very own CD, *Kitten with a Wit*. Check her out at elvirakurt.com.

Comedian **Cathy Ladman** has appeared on *The Tonight Show* a bazillion times, played a recurring character on *Caroline in the City*, and has appeared on *Just Shoot Me*.

Maura Lake is an actress and comedian who has appeared on *Days of Our Lives* and *The Bold and the Beautiful*. She is also a graduate of the Groundlings Theater.

Beth Lapides is the creator of the Un-Cabaret and has performed in and produced the Un-Cabaret touring company, Comedy Central special, and CD. Check her out at uncabaret.com.

Roxane Larimore is the proud winner of the Cleveland Pridefest Laugh Out Proud contest.

Lynn Lavner has taken her original brand of music and comedy to forty-one states and seven countries. Check her out at geocities.com/llavner/

Comedian **Thyra Lees-Smith** lives in Los Angeles and performs in many local clubs, including the Improv and the Comedy Store.

Comedian **Carol Leifer** has been a producer on *Seinfeld,* the star of her own sitcom, *Alright Already,* and is a judge on the new *Star Search.*

LeMaire has appeared on *The Caroline Rhea Show, The Tonight Show,* and on Comedy Central's *Make Me Laugh.*

Wendy Liebman has appeared on *The Tonight Show* and in her own HBO comedy special, and she won an American Comedy Award. Check her out at wendyliebman.com.

Shirley Lipner is a comedian who has been the warm-up for the TBN shows *Rocky Road, Safe at Home,* and *Down to Earth.*

Penelope Lombard tours clubs and colleges around the country and has been seen in numerous TV appearances including on Comedy Central.

Leighann Lord has appeared on Comedy Central's *Premium Blend,* NBC's *Comedy Showcase,* and ABC's *The View.* Leighann has won a Best Actress award in the Riant Theatre Play Festival for her one-woman show, *The Full Swanky,* and won the New York City Black Comedy Award as the Most Thought Provoking Female Comic. Check her out at leighannlord.com.

Susie Loucks has appeared on A&E's *Evening at the Improv, Caroline's Comedy Hour,* and an impressive number of other comedy shows.

Loni Love has appeared on *Star Search,* Fox's *The Best Damn Sports Show Period,* and BET's *Comic View.*

S. Rachel Lovey has appeared on Comedy Central and Fox's *Sunday Funnies,* and she has opened for B. B. King and the Voo Doo Daddies.

Cecile Lubrani is an actress and comedian who has performed at the Comedy Store and the Improv in Hollywood.

Tanya Luckerath is a comedian and actress who appeared in the movie *Beg, Borrow and Steel* and the TV comedy show *Clip Joint.*

Comedian **Bernadette Luckett** has been a staff writer on the sitcoms *Girlfriends* and *Sister, Sister.*

Marla Lukofsky is a twenty-year Canadian comedy veteran and voice-over artist.

Hellura Lyle is a Los Angeles–based comedian and domestic-violence peer who performs on the CD *Comedy Stand Up against Domestic Violence.*

In a career that spanned fifty years, **Moms Mabley**'s performances ranged from the Cotton Club and the Apollo Theater to Carnegie Hall. She recorded nine very popular comedy albums for Chess Records.

Tracey MacDonald is the first Canadian female stand-up comedian to become a *Star Search* grand champion. Check her out at traceymacdonald.com.

Comedian **Kathleen Madigan** won an American Comedy Award for Best Female Stand-up and starred in her very own HBO *Comedy Half Hour.* Her album *Kathleen Madigan* is available from Uproar Entertainment. Check her out at: kathleenmadigan.com.

Kelly Maguire is an actress and comedian who has performed at the Comedy Store and the Improv in Hollywood, participated in the Aspen Comedy Festival, and won a Dramalogue Award for Best Actress. Her recent film credits include *Stranger in My House* for Lifetime television.

Meg Maly and her partner, Blamo, are one of the few male-female stand-up comedy teams. Check them out at funnysincebirth.com.

Lisa Mannerkoski is an actress and comedian who has performed at the Improv in Hollywood.

Comedian **Henriette Mantel** has appeared in *The Brady Bunch Movie, A Very Brady Sequel,* and *The Animal.*

Marilyn is featured on the CD *Hot & Spicy Mamitas of Comedy.*

Melissa Maroff is a Los Angeles–based comedian and the second-place winner of the Far Rockaway Trivia contest.

Monique Marvez's signature raunchy wit and sexualized sarcasm is showcased on her CD, *Built for Comfort.*

Kate Mason is a comedian who plays clubs and colleges everywhere.

Comedian **Sabrina Matthews** has performed at the Montreal Just for Laughs Festival and has been featured on Comedy Central's *Out There in Hollywood* as well as in her own Comedy Central special. Check her out at sabrinamatthews.com.

Comedian **Etta May** has appeared on Showtime's *Aspen Comedy Festival.*

Comedian **Denise McCanles** is a reporter for *LesbiaNation* and has appeared on the syndicated TV show *Night Stand.*

Laurie McDermott has appeared all over Australia, London, and New Zealand. Laurie has been seen on dozens of commercials and international television shows, and she is a humor columnist for *Bride Magazine.* Check her out at lauriemcdermott.com.

Bonnie McFarlane is a Canadian comedian who has played at Yuk Yuk's comedy club.

Kris McGaha hosted sixty-five episodes of MTV's *Loveline,* and her other television appearances include *The Tonight Show* and HBO's *Curb Your Enthusiasm.* Kris also created and starred in the short mockumentary film *Following Tildy.* Check her out at krismcgaha.com

Maria Menozzi is a writer, actress, and stand-up comedian who performs across the country. She is also the author of an award-winning children's play, "The Poet Who Wouldn't Be King." Check her out at ironuterus.com.

Felicia Michaels has won an American Comedy Award and has released her own CD, *Lewd Awakenings*. Check her out at feliciamichaels.com.

Cathryn Michon is a stand-up comedian who has been featured at the Montreal Comedy Festival. Cathryn has also written for a number of TV series and is author of the book *The Grrl Genius Guide to Life*.

Comedian **Beverly Mickins** has had a recurring role on *Judging Amy* and has also appeared on *Thirtysomething*.

Comedian **Stephanie Miller** survived her own *Stephanie Miller Show* on Fox to costar on an MSNBC talk show.

Anita Milner is a lawyer, stand-up comedian, and keynote speaker who enrolled in law school in her forties, passed the California bar exam at age fifty, and celebrated her sixtieth birthday by performing stand-up comedy in Debbie Reynolds' lounge show in Las Vegas.

C. Lynn Mitchell has performed at the Comedy Store and the Improv in Hollywood but recently moved from California to Oklahoma on her own personal "Grapes of Wrath" comedy tour. "Wherever there's a microphone and a drunken, semiconscious audience, I'll be there." Contact: CLynnLaugh@aol.com.

Comedian **Carol Montgomery** has appeared on *Evening at the Improv*, Showtime's *Comedy Club Network*, and *Girls' Night Out*.

Lynda Montgomery has appeared on VH-1's *Spotlight* but considers the highlight of her career to be her performance at the 1993 March on Washington in front of an audience of an estimated one million people.

Nancy Mura has been the host of the *Fox Clubhouse* and has also appeared on A&E's *Evening at the Improv* and *Girls' Night Out*.

After **Christy Murphy** became a finalist in Comedy Central's Don't Quit Your Day Job contest, she quit her day job.

Maureen Murphy has appeared on *The Tonight Show* and in the *Girls of the Comedy Store* video.

Comedian **Sue Murphy** is the star of her own Comedy Central special. Check her out at suemurphycomedy.com.

Rebecca Nell is an actress, writer, and comedian who has performed at a number of Los Angeles clubs, including the Comedy Store.

Leslie Nesbitt has contributed to Bill Maher's monologues for *Politically Incorrect* and she has also appeared on Comedy Central's *Make Me Laugh*. Check her out at leslienesbitt.com.

In addition to stand-up, **Jackie Newton** has been a keynote speaker for the state International Reading Association meetings for Missouri and has developed a K–12 assembly program for schools, Youth Against Violence. Check her out at jackienewton.com.

Comedian **Diane Nichols** has been named "a Queen of Comedy" and "the heroine of the 9 to 5 crowd" by *Newsweek*.

Lydia Nicole has appeared in the movies *Stand and Deliver* and *Indecent Proposal* and on the CD *Hot & Spicy Mamitas of Comedy*.

Susan Norfleet is a *Tonight Show* regular who has also appeared on *The Rosie O'Donnell Show* and *Ellen*.

Rosie O'Donnell has hosted her own cheery talk show and has been featured in movies that include *Sleepless in Seattle* and *Exit to Eden*.

Despite her humble origins in the Rubber Capital of Akron, Ohio, comedian **Ann Oelschlager** has risen to great success in the City of Angels, where she lives in an apartment building with a swimming pool.

Christine O'Rourke is a screenwriter and comedian who performs at the Improv in Hollywood.

Tamayo Otsuki has performed comedy on the Playboy Channel, *Evening at the Improv*, Showtime's *Comedy Club Network*, and in the movie *Don't Be a Menace to South Central*.

Lang Parker has been on NBC's *Last Comic Standing*. Check her out at langparker.com.

Comedian **Maria Parkinson** has appeared on *The Wonder Years,* and her commercial credits include Lexus, Game Boy, and Tropicana Twister.

Nancy Patterson has performed at Stanford & Son's Comedy House, the Cleveland Improv, Bocanuts in Boca Raton, Florida, and at the Cabaret Dada improvisational theater.

Minnie Pearl, a member of the Grand Ole Opry cast from 1940 until her death in 1996, was country music's preeminent comedian.

Dina Pearlman has appeared on Comedy Central's *Premium Blend* and HBO's *Sex and the City.*

Becky Pedigo has appeared on Comedy Central's *Premium Blend.*

Elaine Pelino is a former Texas beauty queen who turned into a stand-up comedian when she realized, "Wow, getting laughs is like being on a really great date—and I didn't even have to remove my pantyhose."

Shawn Pelofsky has performed as an opening act for Bill Maher and Richard Lewis and has been featured at the Montreal Just for Laughs Festival. Check her out at hahachick.com.

Nancy Jo Perdue is a stand-up comedian and Seattle-based journalist.

Mary Pfeiffer is a self-described squeaky-clean comedian. Contact: MerryPfeiffer@webtv.net.

Comedian **Monica Piper** won a Golden Globe for her writing on the sitcom *Roseanne* and her Showtime special, *Monica, Just You,* was nominated for a Cable ACE award.

Marilyn Pittman has two thriving showbiz careers, as stand-up comedian, and producer and host of several nationally syndicated radio shows for National Public Radio.

Brenda Pontiff costarred on the sitcom *The Five Mrs. Buchanans* and has performed as a comedian at the Improv, the Comedy Store, and the Laugh Factory.

Jennifer Post is a stand-up comedian and lawyer.

Comedian **Paula Poundstone** has starred in a number of her own HBO comedy specials.

Chantel Rae has performed at the Comedy Store and the Laugh Factory in Los Angeles, and at the Irvine Improv.

Comedian **Georgia Ragsdale**'s videos include *Sporty Girls* and *Honey Pass that Around,* and her CD is titled *Always Forward, Never Straight.* Check her out at georgiaragsdale.net.

Melanie Reno has appeared on Comedy Central's *Premium Blend.* Check her out at melaniereno.com.

Caroline Rhea has starred on *Sabrina the Teenage Witch* and, call out the coincidence police, has been the host of *The Caroline Rhea Show.* Check her out at carolinerhea.com.

Andi Rhoads is a Los Angeles comedian who has performed at the Improv and the Comedy Store in Hollywood.

Comedian **Karen Ripley** has been performing as an out lesbian since 1977 and has appeared on Comedy Central's *The Daily Show.* Check her out at karenripley.com.

Joan Rivers is a comedian whose career stretches over four decades, an actress, talk-show host, best-selling author, and commentator for *E! Style.* Check her out at joanrivers.com.

Denise Munro Robb has been seen on A&E, Lifetime, Comedy Central, and MTV, and she is a political activist who ran for the Los Angeles City Council. Robb recently got married and came to the realization that she doesn't need a man in her life to make her happy. She can be miserable either way. Check her out at denisemunrorobb.com.

Robin Roberts hosts and produces the critically acclaimed Los Angeles stand-up show "Comedy Schmomedy." Her satirical songs have been featured on the CDs *Comedy Stand Up against Domestic Violence I & II.* Check her out at comedyschmomedy.com.

Roberta Rockwell has been featured in the Toyota Comedy Festival and the Bud Light Ladies of Laughter, and she has been a semifinalist in the Gilda's Club Laugh-Off. Contact: rockwell@nyc.rr.com.

Janet Rosen has been featured in the Marshall's Women in Comedy Festival, has written for *Glamour* and other national magazines, and lives and commits comedy in New York City.

Flash Rosenberg is a comedian and cartoonist who has performed at the Toyota Comedy Festival and the Joseph Papp Public Theater. Flash was also voted Philadelphia's Local Comedian Most Likely to Make You Laugh until It Hurts, and her cartoons have appeared in the *New York Times.*

Comedian **Rita Rudner** has appeared on *The Tonight Show,* has been featured on any number of comedy specials, including her own on HBO, and is author of the books *Naked beneath My Clothes* and *Tickled Pink.* Check her out at ritafunny.com.

Hijiri Sakakibara is an actress and stand-up comedian who has performed at the Improv in Hollywood.

Comedian **Betsy Salkind** has been a writer for the now-syndicated sitcom *Roseanne* and has appeared on *Arli$$* and *The Tonight Show.* Check her out at betsysalkind.com.

Comedian **Charisse Savarin** has appeared on Fox's *The Sunday Comics.*

Stephanie Schiern is a lawyer and a stand-up comedian who has performed at the Comedy Store in Hollywood.

Lisa Schroeer is pursuing a career in public policy while spending her free time enjoying comedy of all sorts.

Liz Sells is a breast-cancer survivor and stand-up comedian.

Sandi Selvi is a wife and mother who triumphed over multiple sclerosis, and a comedian who performs extensively in the San Francisco area and at the Improv in San Jose. Check her out sandiselvi.com.

Sonya Sharpshire is a corporate consultant and a semifinalist in the World Series of Comedy at the Funny Bone in Pittsburgh. Contact: Sharpshire@aol.com.

Comedian **Jennifer Siegal** has worked as a Disneyland portrait artist, dot-com illustrator, and movie critic. On weekends, she likes to go where the green lights take her.

Laura Silverman's was the voice of the bored receptionist, Laura, on Comedy Central's *Dr. Katz, Professional Therapist,* and she appeared in the movie *Half Baked.*

Sarah Silverman appeared in *There's Something about Mary,* played a comedy writer on HBO's *Larry Sanders Show,* and was a comedy writer for *Saturday Night Live.*

Comedian **Carol Siskind** has appeared on *Evening at the Improv, Comic Strip Live, Girls' Night Out,* and innumerable other comedy specials.

Traci Skene is a stand-up comic who is the cocreator, editor, and publisher of SHECKYmagazine.com.

Tony Slaughter is a female comedian who performs at conventions and churches.

Kelly Smith is a comedian and speaker residing in Michigan. Contact: kelly42612003@yahoo.com.

Comedian **Margaret Smith** won an American Comedy Award, taped her own Comedy Central special, and starred in *That '80s Show.*

Tracy Smith has appeared on MTV's *Half Hour Comedy Hour* and Lifetime's *Girls' Night Out.*

Carrie Snow is a stand-up comedian who was a writer on the first two *Roseanne* shows, the sitcom and the talk show.

Wendy Spero has performed on Comedy Central's *Premium Blend.*

Livia Squires has appeared on Showtime. She has been a finalist in California's Funniest Female Contest and appears regularly at the Ice House in Pasadena, California. Check her out at roadcomic.com.

Cyndi Stiles is a Boston-area comedian who has appeared on the bill with comedians Bill Braudis, Teddy Bergeron, and Jen Trainor. Contact: tarn707@comcast.net.

Pam Stone has costarred on the sitcom *Coach* and appeared on *The Tonight Show with Jay Leno.*

Lisa Sundstedt has been a featured performer in the Montreal Just for Laughs Festival and a guest star on *Tracy Takes On.*

Comedian **Sunset** also has performed as the opening act for MUSIQ, Soulchild, and jazz great Paul Taylor. Check her out at comedy.com/sunset.

Comedian **Wanda Sykes** is the host of Comedy Central's *Premium Blend* and star of her own sitcom, *Wanda.*

Comedian **Kim Tavares** has appeared on BET, on a Paul Rodriguez Showtime special, and on *NYPD Blue.*

In addition to founding her own religion (Judyism), comedian **Judy Tenuta** is a panelist on *The Match Game* and star of the film *Butch Camp* and whose comedy albums include *Space Goddessy.* Check her out at judytenuta.com

Tess has appeared on Comedy Central and *The Jamie Foxx Show* and has been a finalist on NBC's *Last Comic Standing.*

Tig can be seen on Comedy Central's *Premium Blend.*

Comedian **Lily Tomlin** was an original cast member of *Laugh-In,* has acted in such films as *Nashville* and *Orange County,* and has appeared in TV series including *Murphy Brown* and *The West Wing.* Check her out at lilytomlin.com.

Rosie Tran is a cute-as-a-button comedian who has performed at the Comedy Store in Los Angeles. Check her out at rosietran.com.

Vicki Trembly is a stand-up comedian, writer, and improv actor who tours the country with her Cranial Aerobics show, spreading joy and silliness whereever she goes. Check her out at cranialaerobics.com.

Jill Turnbow has appeared on *Evening at the Improv, Comedy on the Road, Comedy Club Network,* and *Girls' Night Out.*

Aisha Tyler has appeared on NBC's *Comedy Showcase* and *Friends* and hosted E! Channel's *Talk Soup.* Check her out at aishatyler.com.

Robin Tyler's 1978 comedy album, *Always a Bridesmaid, Never a Groom,* may have been her third album but it was her first as an openly lesbian comic. And in 1979 Tyler became the first openly gay comedian to appear on national television.

Sheryl Underwood has appeared on BET's *Comic View,* on Comedy Central, and in the movie *Bulworth.*

Jennifer Vally has performed in comedy clubs across the United States and worked as a comedy writer and producer for the *Late Late Show with Craig Kilborn, The Tonight Show,* and the Oxygen Network.

Cheril Vendetti has appeared on such TV shows as A&E's *Evening at the Improv* and *Girls' Night Out* and has played comedy clubs across the country.

Tami Vernekoff has appeared on Comedy Central's *Premium Blend* and is a member of the Fashion Police for *US* magazine.

Comedian **Luda Vika** has appeared on all the TV shows that celebrate comedy tonality—*Comedy Compadres, Loco Slam,* and *In Living Color.*

Nancy Waite is a member of the Hyena Comedy Institute All-Stars troupe. Contact: waiten4u2@yahoo.com.

Lesley Wake is a comedian and staff writer for the WB show *What I Like about You.*

Christina Walkinshaw is a Canadian comedian and regular at Yuk Yuk's who is performing in Los Angeles. Contact: walklishus@hotmail.com.

Comedian **Marsha Warfield** played bailiff Roz Russell on the sitcom *Night Court* and later joined the cast of *Empty Nest.*

In addition to her stand-up and sketch comedy work, **Jayne Warren** is an actor and writer. In her spare time, Jayne worries. A lot.

Lotus Weinstock was a beloved Los Angeles comedian whose career spanned three decades, from her engagement to Lenny Bruce to appearances on *The Tonight Show, Evening at the Improv,* Lifetime's *Girls' Night Out,* and her extensive charity work.

Cindee Weiss has performed at the New York Comedy Club, the Comedy Cellar, Gotham City Improv, Stand-Up NY, and Yuk Yuk's in Toronto.

Mercedes Wence is a Los Angeles–based comedian.

Sheila Wenz has appeared on the cable channels Lifetime, A&E, and Comedy Central.

Comedian **Suzanne Westenhoefer** is the star of her own HBO special and a CD titled *Nothing in My Closet but My Clothes.* Check her out at suzannew.com.

Comedian **Penny Wiggins** has appeared on Showtime's *Rude Awakenings* and *The Tonight Show with Jay Leno.*

Jeanne Wiley has been featured in the book *A Funny Time to Be Gay.*

Wendy Wilkins has been seen on MTV, Showtime, and HBO's *Mr. Show.*

Comedian **Karen Williams** has performed in PBS's *In the Life* and her material has been featured in *Out, Loud & Laughing.*

Comedian **Lizz Winstead** is the creator of Comedy Central's *The Daily Show* and—God help us all—*The Man Show*.

Comedian **Anita Wise** has appeared on *The Tonight Show* and at the Just for Laughs Festival in Montreal.

Jackie Wollner has been a finalist in the prestigious San Francisco Comedy Competition, and is the creator of "You Animal You—A One Mammal Show."

UK comic and actress **Victoria Wood** has appeared on a number of British TV shows and released her own video, *As Seen on TV*.

Pamela Yager has appeared on *Saturday Night Live* and Comedy Central's *Stand-Up, Stand-Up*. Check her out at home.earthlink.net/~pyager/.

Donna Jean Young was a comedian of the 1960s who was featured on *Laugh-In* and in her own comedy album, *Live from East McKeesport*.

When **Kate Zannoni** isn't in a carpool, camping with the Cub Scouts, or serving Pop-Tarts for dinner, she's a stand-up comic in Cleveland, Ohio.

uBu (ibme) Zurub has performed at the Hollywood Improv, Caroline's in New York, and the Cleveland Improv, among other venues. Check her out at comics.comedycircle.com/ubu_zurub.html.